dancing in the storm

Successfully Embracing Change

Linda McGinn Waterman

LAUGHING
GULL
PRESS

©2017 by Linda McGinn Waterman. All rights reserved.

Published by Laughing Gull Press
88 Gillette Place
Murrells Inlet, SC 29576

Originally published in softcover by Fleming H. Revell
©1999 by Linda R. McGinn

Published by Fleming H. Revell
A division of Baker Book House Company
P.O. Box 6287, Grand Rapids, MI 49516-6287

Printed in the United States of America

All rights reserved. No part of this publication may be reproduced, stored in a retrieval system, or transmitted in any form or by any means—for example, electronic, mechanical, photography, recording or otherwise—without the prior written permission of the copyright holder. The only exception is brief quotations in printed reviews.

Unless otherwise marked, Scripture quotations are from the HOLY BIBLE, NEW INTERNATIONAL VERSIONS ®. NIV®. Copyright ©1973, 1978, 1984 by International Bible Society. Used by permission of Zondervan Publishing House. All rights reserved.

Scripture quotations marked TM are from THE MESSAGE. © by Eugene H. Peterson 1993, 1994, 1995. Used by permission of NavPress Publishing Group.

Scripture quotations marked NASB are from the NEW AMERICAN STANDARD BIBLE ®. Copyright © The Lockman Foundation 1960, 1962, 1963, 1968, 1971, 1972, 1973, 1975, 1977, 1995. Used by permission.

Scripture quotations marked NLT are the Holy Bible, New Living Translation, copyright © 1996. Used by permission of Tyndale House Publishers, Inc., Wheaton, IL 60189. All rights reserved.

ISBN 978-0-9986179-0-9
Library of Congress Catalog Card Number: 2017902553

Contents

Acknowledgments   9
Introduction   11

Part 1:   Facing The Chaos
1. Chaos: The Raw Material of Life   15
2. Playing the Games of Resistance: Our Attempts at Chaos Management   29
3. Structuring: Managing Chaos by Trying to Order It   43
4. Going Blind: Managing Chaos by Refusing to See It   49
5. A Step into Sorrow   67

Part 2:   Embracing the Chaos
6. Finding Peace in the Process   83
7. Learning to Let Go: The Act of Giving Up Control   103
8. Integrating Daily Chaos into the Fabric of Life   121
9. Integrating Traumatic Chaos into the Fabric of Life   135
10. Integrating Chaos through Change Management in the Workplace   155
11. Finding Rest in the Midst of Chaos   173

The Chaos Factor: Seven Life-Changing Steps for Coping with Chaos   189
Questions for Reflection: The Chaos Factor and You   191
Notes   197

"Look deeper through the telescope and do not be afraid when the stars collide towards the darkness, because sometimes the most beautiful things begin in chaos."
—Robert M Drake

Acknowledgments

Warmest thanks to the following friends who have encouraged me in the midst of chaos.

Jennifer Tubbiolo-your outstanding publishing experience and expertise mixed with patience enabled me to move forward in completing this project as my writing and ministry career spans another decade.

Judy Stewart-the insights and wisdom drawn from your counseling knowledge offered new perspective, crystallized my thinking, and challenged me to write a better book.

In memory of the beloved Edna Edwards-your friendly greetings and bright smiles often gave me the courage to go on as I learned to embrace the chaos.

Dennis Hensley-your encouragement keeps me always writing.

T. R. Hollingsworth-my cheerleader, excellent editorial assistant, forever friend and mother.

Ruthie, John, Cera, Amy, John Jr., Caroline and Wyatt (my precious children and grandchildren)-the warmth of your love always lights up my life.

Reen Waterman-my beloved husband whose gift of encouragement and steadfast love keeps me going every day.

My Lord Jesus Christ-who consistently works all the chaos for good in ways that speak life and love eternally.

Introduction

I sit, curled up on the couch, enjoying the warmth of the fire crackling in the fireplace on an autumn day. Gazing out the picture window of my mountain cabin, I watch the wind tickle and toss leaves dressed in brilliant red, orange, yellow, and green. As they dance with delight, their seemingly random chaos whispers a deeper reality. I begin to wonder why it is that though I find myself safe and warm inside my walls, leaves in the chaos of a bitter wind are dancing. When was the last time I danced?

Chaos. All my life I've feared it. I've sheltered myself behind walls of order, structure, routine, and schedules. These create security and peace. These are the things you can count on when life seems an abstract puzzle. Or so I believed.

Then my life fell apart. Things that seemed certain were suddenly up for grabs. Life was not working the way it should. Structure, routine, and schedules did nothing to protect me from pain.

Maybe you've been there, too. Maybe you've felt the harsh, cold winds of reality pierce your soul like the blinding ice crystals of a blizzard. At such times, nothing seems to make sense. Everything fails you—all your attempts at order, all your plans and systems, and all the coping mechanisms you've carefully devised. You're left with chaos.

Introduction

You have a choice. You can resist the ebb and flow of chaos. You can regroup behind inner walls more impenetrable than fortresses of brick and mortar. Chin up, shoulders back, you force yourself to function so the world will not suspect.

Or you can surrender and make the most daring decision possible. You can accept the chaos. Did I just see you flinch? You're right. It won't be easy. It may even hurt for a while. But the pain will subside, and the richness of life will be yours. You will know joy and hope. And best of all, you will know rest. It's yours for the taking. Only you can make the choice. But I can promise you, if you make the latter choice, life will become an adventure waiting to happen, a mystery ready to unfold. Life will be good. And you will not regret the choice. You will choose it time and time again when chaos confronts you.

If you're willing, you can discover the truth that science, medicine, and business are beginning to prove: chaos forms the very framework of life. Chaos underlies every moment of your existence. Whether it rears up and ravages your life or materializes in more subtle forms—nagging interruptions, unexpected inconveniences, surprise occurrences—chaos is all around you. By accepting rather than resisting it, you can experience the inner peace you crave.

Chaos brings peace? That's what I'm saying. By surrendering to it, you do not drown. Instead you learn to dance with the leaves in the winter wind. Turn the page and join the dance.

Part 1

Facing the Chaos

Chaos

The Raw Material of Life

The real voyage of discovery consists not in seeking new landscapes but in having new eyes.

Marcel Proust

It was my birthday.
I don't know about you, but my birthdays never seem to slip by unnoticed, though I often wish they would. Invariably they become times of reflection, disappointment, or sheer pleasure—but a birthday is never a meaningless marker of time. This one was no different. It was a day that opened my eyes to a new reality and changed me forever. Life would never look the same again.

The day started normally. My husband showered, ate breakfast, and picked up the morning paper as he headed for the office. My three children dressed, gobbled down hot oatmeal with raisins, slung backpacks over their shoulders, and disappeared into the waiting school bus. The day was mine.

Normally I would be off to the office, but today I was free. My birthday. I had decided to celebrate by slowing down, resting, and simply enjoying a day of leisure. That was the plan, anyway.

After a relaxed morning spent reading and answering correspondence, I had a wonderful thought: *Why not call my husband? We could share lunch together. After all, it is my special day. Sure we've been on a tight budget lately, but a little celebrating couldn't hurt, just this once.* I picked up the phone, dialed the number, and heard his voice.

"How about lunch today?" I asked, hoping he'd remember it was my birthday. Lately, he'd been overly busy and had forgotten lots of things.

"I'm sorry," he replied absently. "I'm supposed to meet a client for lunch today. It's an appointment I just can't miss. How about another day this week?"

But another day won't be my birthday. This is the day that matters.

"Okay," I said. I didn't want to be silly about my birthday and let him know his refusal hurt and disappointed me. "See you later."

"Gotta go. See you tonight." Preoccupation was evident in his voice. The receiver clicked off and I found myself standing there holding the buzzing instrument.

Now what? I still wanted to do something special for my birthday, so I dialed a friend's number. My thoughts wandered as I waited. *I really only have one good friend now,* I admitted to myself. *Has it been almost two years since this job transfer carried us away from the Texas friends I loved? And now it's been two months since Carol died.*

Carol. She was more than a friend, more like a soulmate. Her friendship had removed the loneliness caused by lost friends and an increasingly absent husband.

A male voice answered the phone. "Hello?"

"Hi, Mike. Is Sara there?"

"No, Linda. She's with our son Greg. Yesterday, we had to take him to a drug rehab clinic in Chattanooga. He's gotten really bad lately. She's driven over to see him and will be staying for a few days."

"Oh, I'm so sorry to hear that about Greg. I'll talk to Sara later. Thanks." Click. Again the receiver hung in my hand. I'd reached out to touch someone and no one was there.

Waves of sadness rolled over me. I missed my old friends. I missed my husband, whose work was stealing our life and love. I missed my friend Carol, who had been ravaged by cancer and stolen from me. I hurt for Mike and Sara, loving parents who now suffered the agony of a troubled child, agony that seemed so undeserved and unexpected. The unavoidable realities of life gripped me and squeezed the breath out of me.

What happened to "happily ever after"? What happened to the dream I had nurtured for a lifetime: a simple life, neat, orderly, predictable, and safe? The feelings that clenched my soul were more than disappointment or self-pity. I was experiencing something I had never allowed myself to experience before: disillusionment. Disillusionment over life itself and the chaos that seemingly governed it. I felt robbed by unwanted and unexpected events, emotionally ransacked by life's discrepancies. Where was the simple, peaceful, orderly life I believed was my right as a human being?

Misery swept over me like crashing waves, battering my defenses, smashing my coping mechanisms. I was left emotionally bare for the first time. I felt helpless.

Finally, I began to allow myself to grieve—not only for Carol and the months spent watching her die, but for the strangeness of life itself, for the quality of existence that like a wild stallion defies the bridle. It races past all boundaries, unwilling to be tamed. With reckless abandon it moves, free to wreak havoc wherever it wants. I believed in God, the Sovereign Creator. But what control did he have over this wild creature?

I sought peace. I needed answers. I needed a name for this raging stallion. I needed life to have some semblance of sense.

Have you ever been there? Maybe you're there right now. Maybe you've seen how some major tragedy tears at your life, or maybe it's just a collection of minor events that shake you. In any case, life suddenly holds more questions than answers and you *need* the answers. Maybe not all the answers just yet, but at least enough to go on.

Chaos Is Its Name

Chaos.
That's the stallion's name. This is the wildness that breaks through your barriers, calling everything into question. Everywhere you go, this bronco bucks in the background. You can try to ignore it for a while, but it will not be disregarded forever. You can try to break it, but it won't be tamed. You can, however, make peace with it. In fact, if you want a truly satisfying life, you must. Your relationship with chaos will help determine whether you live in joy and peace, or turmoil and bitterness.

Chaos actually does us a favor. It smashes the false foundations on which we try to build our lives. "Happily ever after" is a dream. When we begin to depend on it, the dream becomes a nightmare.

Am I a cynic? No. For years, many typed me the eternal optimist. But I have faced the fact that "happily ever after" creates unattainable expectations—a perfect world made up of perfect people and perfect moments, filled with perfect events marching in perfect precision. That's an unreal world.

Look around you. Read the morning paper. See the world as it really is—broken. No, life doesn't hold only bad news, not at all. In the midst of the brokenness we find cherished moments, joyous events, euphoric realizations, and peace. But only as we look at life and the world with *new* eyes. We must be willing to consider new ideas and entertain new thoughts.

And that's what we'll do in this book: acknowledge and examine the chaos that refuses to be silent while it challenges our every moment. We'll evaluate our responses to it, discover new ways to approach it, and manage the changes it demands so we can experience peace in the midst of the chaos. That's what we all desire, isn't it? Peace. And it is possible.

One of Life's Constants

Let's begin by considering life in light of chaos. Life has two primary constants. First, there is God. Few will deny it. Next, there is chaos. It permeates every fiber of our existence.

Think about it. When you awaken in the morning, all the schedules and plans you had for the day mean nothing if a snowstorm hit during the night. Your kids can't go to school. Your car is stuck. You have no electricity. The telephone wires are down. Chaos.

Or your daily routine goes well unless your boss calls a staff meeting. Fine, except your secretary forgets to give you the message. You miss the meeting, earn the wrath of your boss, and lose the promotion you were banking on. Chaos.

Or your four-year college studies provide excellent preparation for your first full-time job—until you discover you're pregnant. Chaos.

I call it the Chaos Factor. It's amazing how we struggle through life either denying or attempting to organize chaos while consciously ignoring its existence. We don't want to believe we are surrounded by chaos. Why? Because it is completely out of our control and, as a result, fearsome. It is important that we recognize not only its existence but the reality that chaos is a given. It cannot be avoided. Does that make you feel uncomfortable or afraid? Probably both. I'm not surprised. There is a reason.

Acknowledging the Fear

Fear is our natural response to chaos. We, as a culture, determined long ago that anything we cannot analyze, categorize, or explain threatens us. We've abandoned the reality of mystery for rationalism, and as a result, fear lurks in the shadows.

I recently came across an ad for Nike shoes. It read:

Fear of Failure
Fear of Success

Fear of Losing Your Health
Fear of Losing Your Mind
Fear of Being Taken Too Seriously
Fear of Not Being Taken Seriously Enough
Fear That You Worry Too Much
Fear That You Don't Worry Enough
Your Mother's Fear You'll Never Marry
Your Father's Fear That You Will

What is Nike's answer to these fears? "Group Therapy from Nike. *Just Do It.*"

Let me suggest that every one of these apprehensions is rooted in a fear of chaos. Each of these statements hints at the unknown. We don't know what the future holds. And as a culture, we also feel threatened by anything we can't predict. Because of the Chaos Factor, all of life's moments are unknown, and Nike shoes won't change that. Everything is uncertain, except God, of course. And that's the most reassuring exception there is.

A great peace comes in knowing that there is a God and that he *is* the God of chaos. At the same time, he's the God who does not change. He says so when describing himself in his book, "Every good and perfect gift is from above, coming down from the Father of the heavenly lights, who does not change like shifting shadows."[1]

His character is constant. His love isn't fickle. His care doesn't falter. In this life of constant change and humanly unpredictable chaos, he can be trusted. And in him we are secure. Because of him, we can face the chaos without fear.

Chaos in Our Midst

As you boldly face the chaos of your life, you can transform it into a positive and productive thing. That may sound impossible, but trust me on this. It can be done. As you read this book and choose to wade into the turbulent stream of chaos, I believe you'll discover some thrills you'll never forget, adventures beyond imagination.

Let's look more closely at what I'm calling the Chaos Factor. I find three principles at work:

1. *Chaos is the raw material from which life is created.* Chaos is not the enemy of God and certainly not his antithesis. It is the basic stuff of his creation. Though we cannot predict or explain it, chaos is not entirely random. The unseen Conductor of life orchestrates the strains of chaos to create the music our souls long to hear.
2. *Our nature is to resist the chaos.* Change is never comfortable. We arch our backs in resistance. The rapid change that chaos brings is disturbing to most of us. We feel pain as a result. But by resisting, we oppose our destiny. God's unique pattern for our lives will emerge from the chaos just as the butterfly bursts from the chrysalis. Joining God in the process by accepting rather than resisting the chaos brings peace.
3. *In the mystery of chaos, God meets us and we find rest.* Though we create elaborate methods and systems to deny or eliminate chaos, it remains. And in the midst of it, God reveals himself to us. But are we looking for him there? If we keep denying or resisting the chaos, we'll miss out on the secrets God offers.

The Raw Material of Life

My dictionary defines chaos as "a state of things in which chance is supreme; the confused unorganized state of primordial matter before the creation of distinct forms . . . the inherent unpredictability in the behavior of a natural system (as the atmosphere, boiling water, or the beat of a heart)."

I find this definition helpful but incomplete. First, consider "the confused, unorganized state of primordial matter before the creation of distinct forms." I assume these words refer to the Bible's creation account: "In the beginning God created the heavens and the earth. Now the earth was formless and empty."[2]

First, who determined that primordial matter was confused or unorganized?

Second, the definition assumes that chaos was some original problem God fixed by creating the heavens and the earth. But then where did chaos come from? Doesn't it make more sense to say that God created this primordial chaos as the raw material from which he then fashioned the heavens and earth? If so, chaos is as fundamental to our life as the air we breathe and the food we eat.

Third, my dictionary not only calls chaos "a state of things in which chance is supreme" but defines chance as "apparent absence of cause or design." But as one who believes in the Master Designer, I don't believe there can be an absence of cause or design. *Apparent* is the key word—what appears to be chance proves instead to be a divinely orchestrated design.

The studies of John Briggs and F. David Peat concur with this belief. In their book *Turbulent Mirror: An Illustrated Guide to Chaos Theory and the Science of Wholeness,* they write,

> Chaos, irregularity, unpredictability. Could it be that such things are not mere noise but have laws of their own? This is what some scientists are now learning. More than that, these scientists are showing how the strange laws of chaos lie behind many if not most of the things we consider remarkable about our world: the human heart beat and human thoughts, clouds, storms, the structure of galaxies, the creation of a poem, the rise and fall of the gypsy moth caterpillar population, the spread of forest fire, a winding coastline . . . the Christian creator *Himself* is chaos as much as he is order. God is the whirlwind, the fiery destruction, the deliverer of plagues and floods. Apparently to be a creator requires operating in a shadowy boundary line between order and chaos.[3]

Finally, our definition states that chaos is "the inherent unpredictability in the behavior of a natural system." Unpredictable to whom? To humans, certainly. But from the Creator's perspective, nothing is confused, unorganized, or random. Chaos may defy human prediction, but who is to say it escapes divine design? It seems most certainly governed by the Creator's care.

Astounding Discoveries

Briggs and Peat aren't the only scientific sleuths on the trail of chaos. The last twenty years have seen great interest in chaos theory within the science community, though few in the general public are aware of it.

In 1975 a meteorologist made an amazing discovery. Experimenting with his new computer, Edward Lorenz of the Massachusetts Institute of Technology began programming weather models. He expected them to repeat themselves with Newtonian predictability. Centuries ago Isaac Newton had established the theory that all matter is a closed system: nothing from the outside interferes, and everything is governed by sequential order.

In other words, things occur in a predictable manner. One plus one always equals two. Newton's way of looking at life was linear, with no room for surprises. In math—and in meteorology—that meant certain patterns would recur without variation. That's what Lorenz expected to find as he tinkered with his new computer.

But one day he took a shortcut. As he typed in the statistics of the weather models he was trying to duplicate, he rounded off a few numbers—0.506 instead of 0.506127—a change so small that Lorenz didn't think it would make any difference.

It did.

The results floored the scientist. When each of the two numbers was separately multiplied, the patterns that resulted were radically different. The ten-thousandth that had separated the original statistic from the rounded-off version had amplified with every multiplication, creating a vastly divergent result. One seemingly imperceptible alteration had changed everything.

From this accident, Lorenz came up with what he called the Butterfly Effect. A butterfly flapping its wings in Bali can change the wind pattern enough to cause another change, which causes another change, and so on, eventually causing a storm to hit Kansas a few days later. In other words, he proved that life isn't as predictable as we think. The smallest change can make a profound impact.

And so chaos theory was born. As one reporter defined it, "The smallest change in a single variable can have a huge, sometimes catastrophic effect on the whole. A child's shout can start an avalanche. A few particles of ice on an airplane wing can pitch 300 people into Long Island Sound."[4]

Chaos theory asserts that every one plus one doesn't necessarily equal two. One orange plus one orange equals two oranges—unless your child scavenges through the refrigerator after school and decides to eat one. That's the unexpected intervention of chaos. The drive from home to your office may take ten minutes, allowing you time to prepare for your morning appointment—unless road construction forces a detour and an hour's delay. Your problem with alcohol has a beginning, middle, and end as you work through recovery—unless an aunt you're visiting offers you a drink, and you yield to the temptation. Any of these seemingly minor changes can alter the entire flow of events in your life and the lives of those you touch.

Maybe Chaos Is Not So Chaotic

Lorenz demonstrated that weather (and life!) is unpredictable because it's affected by a zillion minuscule changes too plentiful to track. Does this mean the events of our lives are entirely random, without order? On the contrary. Hidden within these seemingly chaotic changes is a remarkably intricate design. This is the second aspect of chaos theory, and it will be of special interest to us.

"Within Lorenz's weather model, he saw an exquisite geometric structure," our reporter notes. "The randomness of his Butterfly Effect was really *order masquerading as chaos*."[5] Beneath this raw material of human existence is an elaborate and amazing pattern, as delicate and breathtaking as a spider's web laden with dew, glistening in the morning sun.

Many years later, highly developed computers proved what Lorenz could not see. The patterns of chaos displayed themselves in vibrant form. Nonlinear systems suddenly mapped the irregular coastline of reality. These findings underscored the point: chaos, though humanly unpredictable, is not random. The pattern of events may be so complex that even the best scientists can't determine it in advance, but that doesn't mean it is without design.

Reporting on the subject, Tim McCarthy wrote, "Within the inherently unpredictable were patterns altogether predictable, faithfully reproduced in every part no matter to what degree they were magnified, and often with astonishing beauty."[6]

The Hidden Pattern of Your Chaos

What does chaos theory mean to you?

First, it means chaos is constantly altering your life. Whether the nuisance of an inconvenient telephone call or the tragic announcement of a spouse's death, chaos interjects new, often imperceptible changes into your daily life. In accordance with the Butterfly Effect, these changes evolve like a snowball rolling downhill, transforming your entire existence.

In a mystery we are beginning to unravel, the truth is that the often unwelcome, unanticipated assault of chaotic intervention in the mainstream of life may be a hidden blessing. When chaotic events collide with our chaotic lives, the Creator himself creates beauty out of the raw material of our chaos.

If this is true, it could change your view of chaos, couldn't it? It could no longer be a dreaded unknown but an acceptable reality of life, something to be expected. You could actually prepare for its inevitability and then learn to embrace it. Particularly when you knew something beautiful would be the ultimate result.

"*What? Are you crazy? Accept, even appreciate, chaos?*" I can hear you now. If you'd said these same things to me ten years ago I'd probably have given you the same response. But I've learned chaos can be understood and eventually accepted and appreciated. What alternative is there but to understand it and decide what to do with it? Are the coping mechanisms you've developed throughout a lifetime protecting you from the disruption of chaos? I can promise you they aren't and won't. They only hide its reality. Chaos is in the weave of life's fabric. So why not learn how to remove the fear, accept it, and even anticipate it?

In the Bible we read, "God causes all things to work together for good to those who love God, to those who are called according to His purpose."[7] You may know that verse well, but in light of chaos theory, the word *all* carries implications we are only beginning to explore. It appears that the things that throw our lives into chaos are actually woven together by a loving God with a purpose. We can't always predict or explain what will happen, but we know the Designer is at work, working it all together in his intricate patterns. Aren't these words basically an ancient statement of what the chaos scientists are only now discovering?

> Step 1: Acknowledge that chaos is the raw material of life.

Accepting the Challenge

Take a moment now and reflect. I began this book by describing life events that forced me to acknowledge chaos. Have you experienced similar events? Throughout this book, I will share

Chaos: The Raw Material of Life

a journey that will enable you to evaluate the chaos in your life and reveal seven revolutionary steps I discovered for coping with chaos, steps I call the Chaos Factor.

We'll discuss these and apply them in simple effective ways to equip us to respond to the chaos in new ways, ways that offer great benefit. We've already started by exploring the first step: acknowledge that chaos is the raw material of life.

We've established that chaos exists. There's not much we can do about that. Infiltrating our lives, it brings multiplied and diverse changes with every new day. Some of these changes are hard to deal with because we don't understand why they happen. But the fact that we can't see a pattern doesn't mean there is no pattern. Science and the Bible teach us that there is order within chaos. If you have chaos in your life, it doesn't mean God is not at work. It means he is.

As we learn to accept that, we can begin to manage the unpredictable changes that chaos brings us. Ultimately, we can find peace.

even
Playing the Games of Resistance

Our Attempts at Chaos Management

Lonely, hollow, shallow, and enslaved to a schedule... Perhaps you have not expressed your world in those words, but they describe why you feel so frustrated, so frayed.

Charles R. Swindoll

Here I am six months after my most memorable birthday. I call it memorable because of its lack of memories. My disillusionment remains. Carol is dead, my husband seems distant in his busyness, no new friends replace those lost in the move. I guess this is exactly what they mean when they talk about a person's life falling apart. Nothing makes sense to me anymore. Hope seems a distant memory and despair my constant companion.

I know all the right things that are supposed to change the picture. I've memorized the Bible verses intended to encourage; I even believe them. But the cloud of apathy and discouragement looms over my head. I feel like the cartoon character Pigpen with a cloud of misery rather than dust surrounding me, but it doesn't feel funny at all.

Shades of pink and white dot the apple and pear trees bursting into bloom at my mother's home in Richmond, Virginia. My father died years ago, and I regularly find solace in her company. Every few years, when the pace grows hectic and life seems out of control, I come here. She and I laughingly call these visits my Richmond Spa experiences. Her home becomes my Betty Ford Rehabilitation Center, though neither alcohol nor drug abuse is my problem. It's a place I go to escape, relax, and regroup, and a time to make sense of the senseless and bring order to the chaos. Time to organize and control the chaos—my methods for chaos management.

What do I do here? Sleep, exercise, eat deliciously prepared low-fat meals—and talk. I pour out the despair of my heart, and Mom gives new perspective. By the end of several days, hope is restored and my systems are back in place.

You see, coping has been our life. My father was what I term a "rage-aholic." The product of an alcoholic home, he never abused alcohol but bore its abusive scars. Rage ordered his world. He controlled the chaos with it. The moment anything displeased him, anger disciplined the offender. Scathing words of hostility or sheer hatred flew throughout the house. What did we do, my mother, brother, and I? Tiptoed lightly and braced for the worst. Life was a vicious cycle of anticipating the unexpected. Yes, the rage was expected, but we never knew what act would trigger the rage—and it was always a hair trigger.

Don't think I didn't love my dad. I did. He was known by the community as honest, friendly, successful, intelligent, even witty, and he was. But my love was always tempered by fear forced to pose as respect. It was demanded. And the dance went on.

We coped with the chaos of my father's behavior by following his lead: control. He controlled the insecurities that ate at his soul by ordering everything and everyone that touched his life. Every moment of every day was clocked to the second. He awakened at 5:15 A.M. We all assembled at the breakfast table by 6:15, according to the unspoken ritual. He left for work at precisely 7:00.

Our evening schedule demanded the same precision. Did the allotted times ever change? Never in my memory. My mother marveled that, even after my father achieved his much awaited retirement, he followed the same exacting schedule until his instantaneous death from a massive heart attack. He was only sixty-three. So young. Such a weary, battered heart. The rage finally destroyed its captive.

So order became my ally. Structure, plans, lists, and programs—these all managed to muffle the cry of insecurity that the chaos aroused. When life became too difficult, I created a strategy to make it work. Change this. Rearrange that. Anything to restore the illusion of security. My motto: Keep the peace at any price.

But here I was, back at the Richmond Spa. My strategies weren't working. Too many chaotic assaults from too many sides had left me unprotected and afraid. All my mother's encouragement, advice, and plans didn't suffice, either. She and I were helpless to fix it.

You see, that was always the goal—fix the mess. Manage it. Control it. Force it into some semblance of order . . . and go on. Blind yourself to the fact that ordering it didn't remove it and guaranteed nothing. Refuse to admit that all the plans, programs, and schedules posed only the illusion of safety. Believe. Have faith. Everything will be all right. But this belief system stood on shaky ground. Was it faith at all? Not really. It was placed in a faulty system of human creation rather than in a God who alone is safe. Disaster always lurked as the ultimate outcome. And disaster had come.

Taking the Step to Realization

I offer this intimate picture so that you might identify with it. How do you cope with chaos? Do you also try to control it by denying it, analyzing it, medicating it, or just keeping a positive attitude? Have you ever reached the point where these strategies stopped working? What did you do then?

That's a painful point to reach, as I discovered. But it puts you on the threshold of a life-changing discovery. Only when you stop resisting the chaos can you face the truth about yourself, about your situation, and about God. Step 2 of the Chaos Factor is to recognize your responses of resistance to chaos and face the truth.

Step 2: Recognize your responses of resistance to chaos and face the truth.

If you want to find rest, you must acknowledge the ways in which you resist or deny chaos. We all resist. We're taught that life should be predictable. Because we are human and gifted with an instinctive fear when danger surfaces, resistance remains our response. When chaos enters life, it is unpredictable, its consequences unknown. So all our predictable, ordered, thinking systems flash alarm lights and blare like the horns of a battleship approached by the enemy, "Warning! Warning! Danger!" Chaos becomes a thing to be feared, an enemy to destroy, a reality to resist.

The sad truth is that chaos in raw form is really neutral. It may result from evil or good, death or birth, penalty or reward, sorrow or celebration, but its existence is not bad. Fear is unnecessary and can actually be detrimental. Why? Because fear triggers a defensive response. Aggression and confrontation result. Then this forceful resistance to chaos begins to define our life.

Researchers are discovering that resistance is a natural response of all creation. Authors Briggs and Peat report, "More and more, researchers are appreciating the way nature has of coupling continuously changing things together in order to end up with systems that effectively *resist* change."[1] Nature apparently works to create resistance to chaos; therefore our resistant responses to chaos are not considered surprising.

The most fascinating aspect of this resistance is the shape it takes. When chaos collides with our self-ordered world, it appears that we respond in one of two ways: by structuring or with blindness. What does that mean? Consider your last chaotic incident. Did you try to restructure the event in such a way that it fit your existing grid? Or did you turn a blind eye to the troubling event that made no sense? Chances are you instinctively took one approach or the other without even thinking about it. Our management systems are so much a part of us, we seldom even recognize them. After acknowledging our innate resistance to chaos, the next crucial step is uncovering the systems we use to resist the chaos.

The Systems That Define You

How about you? What approach do you use to deal with the chaos? When things seem to get out of control, do you whip out your notepad and begin making lists, organizing activities, and restructuring your life to control your environment and manage the chaos?

Or, like Scarlett O'Hara in the epic novel *Gone with the Wind,* do you choose to ignore the existence of chaos? Tomorrow, always tomorrow. You'll deal with it tomorrow.

Let's unveil the two faces of our systems of coping to manage the chaos.

Structure: The Box That Contains Us

Nancy met her chaos with structure. When I met her, I immediately thought she appeared too cheerful and too poised, simply too confident about life. In her mid-thirties and single, Nancy dressed and acted in a manner that announced, "Strictly professional; don't get too close."

Her office decor was perfunctory. The expected plant and pictures of a few relatives stood in place on the bookcase. Most notable was the abundance of clean surfaces. One file strategically lay in the middle of her immaculate desk. From appearances, I suspected her pocketbook had more compartments than contents. She was obviously efficient and in control. Her manner was sterile.

In time, our working relationship revealed more. Nancy laughed too loudly, shook hands too aggressively, and listened too intently. Once I met with her and another coworker to discuss our joint projects. Nancy sat down, read her list of priorities (she always had a list), and exited without ever looking up from her legal pad. She made no eye contact with either of us.

She regularly spoke first and made her point quickly, stating her position as if to say, "Case closed, discussion ended." Trying to relate to Nancy was frustrating. Nothing could ever be undecided. She never left loose ends hanging. I remember she never laughed at herself. Her relationships were shallow because most of us preferred to avoid her. Nancy's contemptuous style of relating left us cold, yet her inner pain seeped through the chiseled hardness of her smile.

Nancy's problem was her lifelong response to chaos. No doubt she'd experienced broken dreams, hurt feelings, betrayed trust—her manner reflected all of these. But when chaos assaulted her, she responded by imposing a rigid structure on every aspect of her life. This way, she could maintain an illusion of control. Plans, projects, appointments, and schedules became the walls that protected her.

Nancy practiced withdrawal—from the confusion, from the pain, from the world in general. By withdrawing, she reduced the number of unpredictable elements in her life. Or so she thought. But her tight reins of control were strangling her one day at a time.

Many of us, like Nancy, respond to chaos with structuring, though few go to that extreme. It's one of our major coping mechanisms when life gets tough.

Blindness as a Coping Strategy

John, on the other hand, retreated from chaos behind blindness. This sixty-something friend spent a lifetime anticipating retirement. He longed for a time when he could bask in the sun on the sandy coastline of Florida. Finally, he realized his dream.

John believed that as long as he stayed fit, death remained a distant future, a foe to be ignored. And so he walked seven miles every day that he didn't play eighteen holes of golf—it was a joyful existence for him.

One day while visiting John and his wife, I noticed he spent all day raking and hauling fallen leaves from his neighbor's yard. He'd agreed to do that for his traveling friends. At three o'clock he entered the living room looking gray and grim—not at all like himself. Startled, I said, "John, sit down. You look sick." He simply stared at me and excused his appearance by mumbling something about the heat.

I remember scolding him—it's thoughtful to help out, but it's sure not worth dying for. He managed a weak smile and disappeared into the bedroom.

Three days after returning home, I received a phone call from John's wife. The previous morning, she said, John had awakened, remarked at the beauty of the day, and set out on his seven-mile walk. Two blocks away, he'd dropped dead from a massive heart attack. The medics were unable to revive him.

I was stunned. Had he been ill? Why didn't he tell us? Had he felt chest pains? If so, why did he keep them a secret?

John's wife later learned that yes, indeed, there had been chest pains. Several weeks before, he had left a golf game to sit in the clubhouse. A friend questioned him, but John said the pains were not serious. When his friend suggested he go to the doctor, John said, "I'll just give it another week or so. If the pain doesn't go away by then, I'll make an appointment."

As weeks passed, his wife recalled other comments John had made. After buying a new watch he remarked, "This is the last watch I'll have to buy." Another time, "You won't have any trouble after I die. The papers are all in order."

He had blinded himself and others to the reality that his death was imminent. "I'll give it another week" were John's words to his golf buddy, typifying John's life. Whenever trouble came, John waited to deal with it later. He feared pain. He feared the possibility of being crippled. He feared death. So he simply pretended it would all go away if he ignored it long enough. Blindness was the coping mechanism that governed his life, and his death.

Are you more like Nancy or John? Do you feel chaos can be controlled through structure, or do you try the Scarlett O'Hara routine: Tomorrow, tomorrow and all will be fine. Most people tend toward one of these two strategies. You can probably see it in the people around you. You can even see it in the pages of the Bible.

Character Pictures

Look at the faces of chaos resistance in the lives of the following individuals. Some are historical figures you will recognize while others are realistic, dramatic portraits of human behavior found in the Bible. As you consider their symptoms of resistance, which ones seem all too familiar in your life?

Anger is a common resistance symptom. Abraham Lincoln recognized its powerful force.

> Abraham Lincoln's secretary of war, Edwin Stanton, had some trouble with a major general who accused him, in abusive terms, of favoritism.
>
> Stanton complained to Lincoln, who suggested that he write the officer a sharp letter. Stanton did so, and showed the strongly

worded missive to the president, who applauded its powerful language: "What are you going to do with it?" he asked.

Surprised at the question, Stanton said, "Send it."

Lincoln shook his head. "You don't want to send that letter," he said. "Put it in the stove. That's what I do when I have written a letter while I am angry. It's a good letter and you had a good time writing it and feel better. Now, burn it, and write another."[2]

Grumbling and complaining are other symptoms that signal resistance. We see the Israelites responding this way in the biblical record of their wilderness wanderings after their escape from Egyptian tyranny.

"When they came to Marah, they could not drink its water because it was bitter. . . . So the people grumbled against Moses. . . . In the desert the whole community grumbled against Moses and Aaron."[3] "The LORD said to Moses and Aaron: 'How long will this wicked community grumble against me? I have heard the complaints of these grumbling Israelites. So tell them, "As surely as I live, declares the LORD, I will do to you the very things I heard you say." ' "[4] Do you ever find yourself grumbling against life's circumstances?

Others couch their chaos resistance in *a longing for the past*. Again, the Bible poignantly portrays our humanity.

When chaos hit Lot's home, God sent deliverance. When Lot hesitated in his escape, "the men [angels] grasped the hands of his wife and of his two daughters and led them safely out of the city, for the LORD was merciful to them." An angel told them, "Flee for your lives! Don't look back, and don't stop anywhere in the plain! Flee to the mountains or you will be swept away!" But Lot's wife looked back, apparently so connected to her old life that she was blinded to the danger and refused to heed the warning. She became a pillar of salt.[5]

When confronted by chaos, do you resist it by clinging to the structures of the past, rather than moving forward into a God-guided future?

Look at some of the other ways we respond to chaos.

Deceit. "On Christopher Columbus's first voyage west, in 1492, his crew was understandably uneasy about the trip through unknown waters to an unknown destination, and for an unknown period of time.

"To reassure the sailors and disguise the true length of the journey, Columbus kept two logs: one of the real distances traveled as he reckoned them, and the other giving shorter ones so that the crew would think they were closer to home than they actually were.

"The irony is that it turned out the falsified figures were more accurate than the ones Columbus kept in the true log."[6]

Blaming others or God. When the chaos of original sin rocked Eden, Adam blamed Eve ("the woman you put here with me") and Eve blamed the serpent.[7] Do you blame others for the situations that rock your life?

Escape (physical, emotional, or intellectual). Jesus' disciples ran away when Jesus was captured before his crucifixion. They chose to blind themselves to the reality of chaos.[8]

Busyness/distraction. Charles Swindoll, author, pastor, and president of Dallas Theological Seminary, describes one pastor's response to chaos, using busyness and distraction as a defense that later proved devastating.

"'Nobody around me knows this, but I'm operating on fumes. I am lonely, hollow, shallow, enslaved to a schedule that never lets up.' As I embraced him and affirmed his vulnerability and honesty, he began to weep with deep, heaving sobs. We prayed before he slipped back into the crowd."[9]

Manipulation of events and people. Sarah's impatience and need to control her situation won out over the faith of her husband, Abraham. When no child arrived in response to God's promise, she solicited a maidservant and convinced her husband to produce a child, structuring an alternative plan. None of their lives was ever the same.[10] Do you tend to manipulate people and manufacture solutions to "fix the mess" chaos makes?

Despair, depression, and questioning God. With the onslaught of chaos in his life, Job questioned his own value and God's purposes.[11] How about you? Do rhetorical questions raised to heaven fly from your lips when you confront chaos in your life?

All of these responses are symptoms of resistance. Resistance produces variations of the two major methods for coping with chaos: structuring and blindness. These symptoms all show an unwillingness to face the chaos head-on. They are attempts to avoid the chaos, and they demonstrate unwillingness to trust the Master Designer to purposefully weave chaos into the fabric of life. Don't feel bad. Everyone uses these systems. You're not alone. But there is freedom in identifying the symptoms, systems, and learning how to respond differently to chaos.

Methods for Chaos Management

Now is your opportunity to discover the personal resistance systems you employ. This quick quiz helps you recognize your typical methods for managing chaos. Though you may feel these systems are indispensable, the reality is that they have kept you from the authentic security and peace that come through integrating chaos into your life.

There are no right or wrong answers to this survey. It's a personal evaluation whose only purpose is to help you see more clearly. Though you may not always experience the feelings or take the actions described, the survey offers clues as to your systems for managing chaos.

(Circle the number that best describes you for each question.)

0—never   1—sometimes   2—frequently   3—always

0 1 2 3   1. Are you more anxious than you think you should be at times?
0 1 2 3   2. Do you have difficulty saying no?
0 1 2 3   3. Do you find that you tend to ignore problems, hoping they will go away?

0 1 2 3   4. Do you avoid feared situations to the point that it interferes with your routine at work, social settings, or in relationships? (Example: to avoid confrontation with another person in the office, you spend extra minutes taking a longer route around the person to reach your destination.)
0 1 2 3   5. Do you have difficulty sleeping or loss of appetite?
0 1 2 3   6. Have you sensed difficulty concentrating or does your mind sometimes go blank?
0 1 2 3   7. Are you reluctant to get involved with people unless you're certain of being liked?
0 1 2 3   8. Are you hesitant to take personal risks or to engage in new activities because they may prove embarrassing?
0 1 2 3   9. Do you struggle with impulsiveness or a failure to plan?
0 1 2 3 10. Do you feel you can never have too much information before making a decision?
0 1 2 3 11. Do you or have you often felt restlessness, a sense of being keyed up, or generally on edge?
0 1 2 3 12. Are you shocked when you hear about an acquaintance's personal struggle?
0 1 2 3 13. When you're down, do you turn on the TV to watch something that might distract you?
0 1 2 3 14. Have you ever wondered if you are abusing alcohol, drugs, or food?
0 1 2 3 15. Do you find yourself daydreaming or imagining you are somewhere else or someone else?
0 1 2 3 16. Do you regularly or often misplace things?
0 1 2 3 17. Do people consider you to be naive?
0 1 2 3 18. Do you have difficulty remembering your childhood?
0 1 2 3 19. Do you suspect you have excessive or unreasonable fear—or do you have panic attacks?
0 1 2 3 20. Are you known as a fanatic cleaner or feel somewhat driven at times to order or check on things?

Playing the Games of Resistance

0 1 2 3 21. Does it bother you (more than you sense it should) when plans or rules change?
0 1 2 3 22. Do you put things off until the last minute or wait until you're in a crisis to act?
0 1 2 3 23. Are you a list maker?
0 1 2 3 24. Would you rather organize your closet than do something creative?

A. Add the numbers circled beside the following questions: 1, 4, 5, 7, 8, 10, 11, 19, 20, 21, 23, 24. Total _____

B. Add the numbers circled beside the following questions: 2, 3, 6, 9, 12, 13, 14, 15, 16, 17, 18, 22. Total _____

If your total for (A) above is higher than (B), your tendency in dealing with chaos is toward the Structure-Formulas System.

If your total for (B) above is higher than (A), your tendency is toward the Chosen Blindness-Naiveté System.

If you found the questions threatening, don't be angry or alarmed. All of us keep returning to these methods for chaos management, even when we know they don't work. Rejecting our systems for God's better way is a process that takes a lifetime to complete. But it starts by understanding our natural coping tendencies and learning how to override them.

In the next chapter, we'll explore the methods of structuring we use for chaos management. Even if this is not your strongest resistance method, you will still gather new insights to enable you to better cope with life and find peace in the midst of chaos.

3

Structuring

Managing Chaos by Trying to Order It

It is difficult to leave behind the familiar past and venture into untraveled territory. So we cling to ideas, habits, and people we should let go of. God knows our needs—even before we recognize them. When we are honest with ourselves and take time to listen inwardly, we know them, too.

Susan L. Taylor

***Imagine** the following* scenario. You have an unmarried teenage daughter who comes home one evening and announces she's pregnant. If you scored high in structuring tendencies, your immediate response would be to organize the chaos. You might decide to send your daughter to Aunt Mary's for the next six months so she can have the baby secretly and put it up for adoption. You'd contact the school, telling them that for medical reasons your teenager must live in Aunt Mary's city, can't attend school, and will need homework assignments to complete in that location. There's no time to pray and seek to know God's will. There's no time to feel your daughter's pain or express your own grief. Your first inclination is to fix the problem—figure out how to make it right. You try to conquer chaos by turning to control and structure.

When methods of control and structure are applied to chaos management, we inevitably distance ourselves from others. Withdrawal becomes essential. Why? Because people and relationships can't be predicted any more than they can be managed. Who knows the human soul but God? And who can anticipate and control the actions of another human being? We avoid this inevitable reality by withdrawing. We make plans and take actions that we assume will prevent any unpredictable elements (usually involving people) from arising. Then we try to control every other imaginable possibility.

The sad fact is that, when we employ structure, we're trusting in our methods of management, not in God. Only he holds the power to manage the chaos for our benefit. But it's our choice: we can rely on our own ineffective control to try to bring about order, or we can trust the infallible God to work through the chaos.

Some things in life are meant to be ordered; others are not. It's one thing to order your checkbook and quite another to apply this same ordering to your relationships. When you use ordering, structure, and formulas as an antidote to chaos, you reveal your fear and hatred of the unknown, of losing control, and of learning difficult truths about yourself.

Examples of Resistance through Structuring

Again, the Bible offers an interesting illustration of structuring as a chaos resistance system. The apostle Peter gave us a graphic demonstration of inappropriate structuring in his response to Jesus' transfiguration.[1] Jesus chose Peter, James, and John to accompany him on a journey up a steep mountain. Suddenly Jesus completely changed. "His clothes became dazzling white, whiter than anyone in the world could bleach them." More terrifying yet, he was speaking with two dead men, Elijah and Moses.

We can only imagine the shock and fear Jesus' companions felt. Peter made a proposition that seems ludicrous. "Let us put up three shelters—one for you, one for Moses and one for Elijah." Peter's immediate need to structure and order this most disquieting moment demonstrates the reflexive devices we turn to in crisis.

Ridiculous? Yes. Understandable? Absolutely. It's comforting to know that we're not alone in our retreat to human devices for chaos management. It's also comforting to know that God has mercy. Look at his response to Peter:

"Then a cloud appeared and enveloped them, and a voice came from the cloud: 'This is my Son, whom I love. Listen to him!'" If a reproach was in order, mercy was the response.

Symptoms of Imbalance

Is it always wrong to make lists, place entries into your day planner, or organize your closet space? No. It's only wrong when you grow to depend on these things for your security. If, when life gets hectic, you find that only sitting down to structure the hours of each day for the coming month allows you to heave a sigh of relief, a warning signal is sounding. Where are you placing trust for management of the chaos? In your feeble plans or in the expertise of the God of the universe?

If you've experienced conflict with a friend and you lie awake at night trying to decide how to control the situation—debating whether to write a letter, ask a friend to intervene, or phone the individual to insist you talk it out—then again you're depending on your own resources to fix the problem.

Motivated more by anger and fear, we impose order and structure in an attempt to ensure control over our world. We want to narrow life to manageable proportions, formulas, structures, and lists. Like Nancy in the previous chapter, we want closure more than we want life.

If, when faced by chaos, we immediately return to old routines, safe environments, and known patterns rather than daring to take risks, we aren't depending on God's supernatural direction and intervention. These responses will not only keep us from him and his successful alternatives, they'll stand in the way of the peace and rest we desperately desire.

Legalism: Our Religious Structuring

Many bring their structuring strategies into their spiritual lives. They fall prey to a set of attitudes and choices we might call legalism.

Often spiritual leaders unwittingly promote legalism. They sincerely want those they direct and instruct to live properly, but they don't entirely trust God's Spirit to guide and direct us. So they play it safe. They demand that we walk a straight and narrow path, one that they construct. They define true spirituality according to a structure of "correct" behavior that must be rigidly followed, rather than as a journey of faith, dependent on God. I call it life on the spiritual tightrope.

Such an approach exchanges passion for lists and purpose for laws. Salvation becomes a product of performance rather than the free gift of the God of intimacy and relationship. Morality becomes a matter of keeping the rules rather than being our loving response to the Divine Lover of our Souls. You must look a certain way, act a certain way, think a certain way.

Max Lucado expresses it this way, "A legalist believes the supreme force behind salvation is you. If you look right, speak right, and belong to the right segment of the right group, you will be saved. The brunt of the responsibility doesn't lie within God; it lies within you. . . . Legalism is slow torture, suffocation of the spirit, amputation of one's dreams. Legalism is just enough religion to keep you, but not enough to nourish you. So you starve."[2]

God does not expect the same of us. Actually, God makes it clear that he knew from the beginning we would be unable to

Structuring

adhere to every command in the Bible. He gave us his Word to provide a picture of himself, his perfection, and his holiness so we could turn to him to find what we cannot secure through our own efforts. He showed us a clear picture of himself through his Son, Jesus Christ, who said clearly, "Be perfect [complete] as your Father in heaven is perfect."[3] That is his standard. Yet he knows that we, being sinners, will fail.

We can see this in the story of the girl and the judge. "In a courtroom one day, a girl came before the judge due to a traffic violation. The law was clear—the judge had to act justly and he fined her 50 dollars for her violation. After pronouncing the sentence the judge excused himself and came down from the bench. Knowing the girl didn't have the $50, he stood beside his precious daughter and paid her penalty, her fine. He then returned to the bench."[4]

Because we are imperfect and live imperfect lives, there is a penalty to be paid, but someone else has willingly paid it for us. Death is the penalty for sin, so Jesus came down and died. When we believe in him, his Spirit frees us from legalism and the dead practice of keeping the law. After all, God knows us better than we know ourselves. He knows our tendency to use self-created coping mechanisms to order life, even our spiritual life. And he knows that if they worked, we would not turn to him. The Bible doesn't contain lists such as Ten Steps to Perfect Parenting or Ten Secrets of the Perfect Marriage. Do you know why? I suspect that if they existed we would use all our structuring methods to fulfill their requirements and never communicate with God again.

Why discuss the spiritual implications of our coping mechanisms so thoroughly? Because when chaos strikes, every time we turn to our old methods, we rob ourselves of a new experience of God's power and love. In essence we choose the sin of trusting our own resources over the safety of trusting God.

The confusion and distress of chaos can feel worse than the sin of organizing God out of our lives, so we choose the sin. Obsession with order keeps us from turning to God. We want to manage rather than trust. And then we end up being swallowed by the muddled mess of chaos.

God *will* show you the way if you ask him. He loves you enough to answer your prayer. He holds you close, waiting for you to trust him in a new way. A new relationship with God awaits you with every revelation. If you will choose to trust God rather than create and rely on self-made structures, new hope and joy in life will be yours. The Divine Director will orchestrate the chaos of your life, and you will hear the sweet strains of a symphony rather than the cacophony of distress.

Thomas Merton, a twentieth-century poet and writer, prayed a prayer of faith that can give us hope as we identify, face, and abandon the permanently flawed coping mechanisms of our lives:

> God, we have no idea where we are going. We do not see the road ahead of us. We cannot know for certain where it will end. Nor do we really know ourselves, and the fact that we think we are following your will does not mean that we are actually doing so.
>
> But we believe that the desire to please you does in fact please you. And we hope we have that desire in all that we are doing. We hope that we will never do anything apart from that desire.
>
> And we know that if we do this you will lead us by the right road, though we may know nothing about it. Therefore, we will trust you always though we may seem to be lost and in the shadow of death. We will not fear, for you are ever with us, and you will never leave us to face our perils alone.[5]

Going Blind

Managing Chaos by Refusing to See It

> Few are the people who don't suffer from some form of blindness.... We can live next to something for a lifetime, but unless we take time to focus on it, it doesn't become a part of our life. Unless we somehow have our blindness lifted, our world is but a black cave.
>
> Max Lucado

Josh is gracious, thoughtful, interested in you. A nicer guy you'll never meet. He goes out of his way to engage you in conversation, intent on remembering the information you share and the concerns you hold. Why? Because he wants to make a good impression. It's important that you like him.

But even after lengthy conversations, you'll know little about Josh. He'll probably disclose the name of his hometown or places he's visited, hoping to find shared interests or mutual friends. That's about it. His primary desire is to know and please you.

When questioned about his home or family, he answers with pride and confidence but quickly turns the subject back to you.

If you ever need anything, Josh is there. He'll do anything to help. You find him thorough, sincere, and considerate. You see, he has to be. It's the way he avoids the pain of his past—a past ridden with shame, guilt, and constant covering for the misery of an alcoholic home.

Josh stuffs the pain, ignores its truth, hides the facts—even from himself. Even in adulthood, he plays the role of image protector. His family members worked hard to appear whole, happy, and normal to the outside world, when in reality they were anything but. That's where he learned to play the part. Don't let anyone know the truth. And what *is* the truth, really? They *were* a loving, happy family, weren't they? Fighting to believe it, he spends his life trying—doing good works to make the image a reality. Anything to make him feel better about himself.

You see, Josh's blindness to the truth about his family has blinded him to the truths about himself. Because he has never faced the facts about his chaotic upbringing, he can't explain the shame he feels deep within. He thinks he cares about you, and maybe in some way he does. But most of all he cares about himself. He spends his life assuaging the guilt, easing the shame, proving the lie that he has believed all his life: the lie that he is worthless. You see, he believes he doesn't deserve happiness or peace. He doesn't deserve your approval or warrant your interest, but if he works hard enough to gain it and you grant it, he may find some value after all.

Josh deserves no blame for his parents' alcoholism or the shame he was forced to bear as a result. He is not worthless. But blindness to the truth is the unspoken language, the demanded pattern. If he accepts his inherent value, he'll have to admit his family messed him up—and that shatters the image that must be preserved at any cost. Unfortunately, the cost is exorbitant.

Sometimes the people closest to Josh feel taken for granted. He doesn't need their approval so much—after all, they already love him. If he doesn't come through for them, they'll understand. And you can't always count on Josh to do what he promises. His constant commitments to others stack up until little time remains in the day to do them all. He never learned to say no.

And whenever he's confronted with these inconsistencies, he doesn't see them. He has chosen not to. He believes blindness rather than love covers a multitude of sins. He can always think about these things tomorrow. Of course, he never does.

Obscuring Our Vision

Josh has always dealt with chaos by choosing blindness. Even now, he refuses to acknowledge his parents' alcoholism. He stubbornly refuses to let anyone enter his life and discover the lie.

Early in his life, Josh created an illusory world to replace the broken one in which he had to live. And he remains in that world today. There's no chaos there. As long as Josh cannot see what he fears or hates, he can assume it doesn't exist. The more he hones his illusion-building skills, the more his imaginary world expands. Until the day comes when chaos intervenes, and it can't be ignored.

Driving while drunk, his dad crashes the car.

The Avon lady peers through the window and sees his mom stretched out on the floor, drunk. Fearing foul play, she calls the police.

Dad loses his job for coming in late when he's hung over, which has been all too often.

Mom shows up at school for a parent-teacher conference with alcohol on her breath and slurred speech.

For a moment, then, Josh is forced to confront the truth about his family, and he can't handle it. After all, he's just a kid. To admit to his family's serious problem leaves him feeling devastated and lost. He fears the future. What will happen to them? And what will this mean about *him?* Will he have serious problems, too? It's all too terrifying to think about, and he chooses not to.

The family conspired to do damage control whenever its problems became public. Preserved the image. And the rest of the community often helped to sweep unfortunate incidents under the rug. Josh preserved his own illusions, too. The chaos usually subsided in a few days or weeks. Once again, they all pretended everything was fine.

Now as an adult, Josh fears his past, so he never talks about it. He fears his true feelings, so he doesn't let himself feel them. He fears that someone will uncover the awful truth that he is worthless and he's going through life faking it. So he keeps the focus on others, winning their approval but avoiding any real relationships. Josh fears that any sort of chaos will topple the house of cards he has carefully constructed. So when anything chaotic enters his life, he does what he's always done—he pretends it doesn't exist.

The Fears That Blind Us

As we see in Josh's story, blindness often results from fear. Afraid to look at the chaos of our lives, we choose not to. So let's examine fear, and that may help us better understand blindness.

Fear entered the world not long after Adam and Eve chose rebellion over obedience. You may remember the scene. God was walking in the cool of the garden looking for the couple. They were hiding.

"The LORD God called to the man, 'Where are you?'

"He answered, 'I heard you in the garden, and I was afraid.'"[1]

What was Adam afraid of? The consequences of their rebellion against God. And God went on to pronounce the penalties for their rebellion. These proclamations are often called "the curse," but notice that fear preceded them. Fear arose before the specifics of the curse were even stated. Adam and Eve knew something would happen to them, but they weren't sure exactly what.

From the beginning God had clearly defined the parameters of life for Adam. Offering him all the bounty of his garden home, "God commanded the man, 'You are free to eat from any tree in the garden; but you must not eat from the tree of the knowledge of good and evil, for when you eat of it you will surely die.'"[2] God spoke the truth to Adam long before Eve or the serpent appeared on the scene. God's protective warning, "you will surely die," prepared him for the inevitable consequences that would follow his rebellion if he chose to eat the forbidden fruit.

The truth was that those consequences would inevitably prove to be deadly both spiritually and physically. Death, the ultimate consequence, lies at the root of all fear. Death is the ultimate out-of-control experience.

God introduced fear into the human heart not to spoil our fun but to alert us to danger. As Don Allender puts it, "God's commands are connected to consequences that produce fear for the purpose of warning us of harm."[3]

Fear can be positive, productive, and protective. Fear makes you look both ways before crossing the street—you're afraid of stepping into the path of an oncoming car. Fear makes you investigate an unfamiliar noise in your darkened basement—you're afraid a burglar may have broken in. You may have felt an inner foreboding when you were about to make a bad choice about something in your life. Your fear warns you about negative consequences of bad actions. Protective fear is God's warning system. God lovingly attaches the strongest possible consequence—death—to allow fear to work positively. His desires are always for our best.

So fear by itself is not the problem. Fear can inspire us to make good choices. But it can also lead us to choose blindness, as we saw in Josh's case. What's the difference?

Say you're working as a security guard and an alarm sounds. You have two choices: investigate or ignore. You could pull some wires and make the alarm stop; that would be choosing blindness. Or you could see what caused the alarm to go off, and then deal with the situation.

When life gets chaotic, it may alarm us. Our fear may lead us in either of two directions. On the path of blindness, we try to ignore the chaos. On the other path, we investigate the chaos and deal with it; this is, of course, the better way.

Fear in the Garden

We see this demonstrated in Genesis 2 and 3 as Eve debates with the serpent. The tempter asks Eve to reject the words of God, convincing Eve to blind herself to reality and believe a lie. "You will not surely die," the serpent says, contradicting God's clear warning. "For God knows that when you eat of it your eyes will be opened, and you will be like God, knowing good and evil."

Ironically, blindness is masquerading as clear vision, as it often does. At some level, Josh thinks denial of his family problems is helping him cope with life. But distortion of truth always seems like truth; that's what makes it so tempting. In Eden the tempter was saying, in essence, "God is deceiving you. He doesn't want your best. He just doesn't want you to be as smart as he is. Forget what God said—see it my way instead. Blind yourself to the truth and listen to me."

The serpent was asking Eve to pull the wires of her God-given alarm system, to put an end to fear by deciding it was unfounded. Ultimately, she did that. Eve's desire won over fear's counsel. As a result, humankind from then until now struggles to discriminate between God-given fear, which leads to wisdom,[4] and Satan's perverted fear, which leads to death.

The Blindness of Shame

Fear is not the only emotion that induces us to choose blindness. Another is shame. We saw a subtle thread of shame woven through Josh's story. Shame is the whole fabric of Angie's story.

A few years ago Angie's life began to fall apart, beginning with her marriage. As a Christian she disapproved of divorce, but her husband's behavior became so outrageous she had to consider it. Her church leaders agreed that she had biblical grounds for divorce, and so she went through with it. Now she must raise her two small children on her own.

Going Blind

One year after the divorce, Angie was diagnosed with breast cancer, which resulted in a mastectomy. And not much later, her ex-husband was arrested in a highly publicized case for robbing three banks of nearly two hundred thousand dollars. The combination of these events terrified Angie. First, she had to face the possibility that she would die, then the horrendous thought that the kids would have to be reared by their criminal father. Even if she survived, Angie would have to struggle to make ends meet after paying medical expenses and getting zero child support from her ex.

The shame was excruciating. Angie found all sorts of reasons to feel bad about herself. She berated herself for marrying her husband in the first place, but then wondered if she was right to divorce him. Was her cancer some form of divine judgment? And if she made such bad choices, what kind of mother could she be? Look, she could hardly put food on the table, much less give her kids any of the material things they deserved.

The shame forced her into a sort of blindness, ignoring the pain of her situation and even the reality of the events that had brought her there. She never talked about her husband or about the cancer, and other people were just as happy to avoid those unpleasant subjects. She told her children little about their dad; instead she created an image of a father who would comfort them, love them. They didn't know he was serving six years in prison for bank robbery.

This method worked wonderfully until the day he was released. Immediately, he visited the children—and nothing has been the same since. Angie was forced to admit to her kids that she'd been deceiving them. Her illusory world evaporated. Once again, she had to face painful reality.

Angie's story depicts blindness in its most obvious form—a continuous refusal to acknowledge the truth. She felt shame about her bad choices and her perceived ineptitude as a wife and mother, and this shame caused her grief. Rather than confronting her pain, she employed various techniques to choose blindness. She avoided talking about painful things and even made up stories to cover the truth.

Yet blindness is not always so obvious. Sometimes it surfaces as a positive attitude, something I call blind optimism. Seemingly harmless, even this can obscure reality. Blind optimism often crashes into misery and disillusionment.

Is a positive attitude bad? Absolutely not. The Bible urges us to think about "whatever is true, whatever is noble, whatever is right, whatever is pure, whatever is lovely, whatever is admirable."[5] There's nothing wrong with focusing on the positive as you face life's chaos and difficulties.

As one greeting card says:

> Optimism is hope in sneakers—it makes life more comfortable but doesn't have to be taken too seriously.
> An optimist looks at the *bright side,* walks on the *sunny side,* and gets up on the *right side* of the bed every day.
> This may lead to the impression that optimists are slightly out of touch, but they are the ones who strike the match that *dispels all the dark.*
> Who else reminds us that a glass half empty is also *a glass half full?*
> Who else looks for the pony wherever there's a pile of you-know-what?
> Who else pictures life *a little rosier* than it is?
> And often, because of them, it really is.

Optimism is a great source of encouragement, but when a positive attitude disguises or distorts the truth, it becomes a tool of blindness and deceit. I've begun to learn that optimism is not the same as hope—and hope is what I want in my life.

I wrote about this in my journal after visiting several cherished friends of the past, one of whom is named Julie.

> Listening to the sad despair of Julie's heart, I realize that due to my grief over Carol's death, my search to understand relationships and why this one meant so much, and my personal need to find God sufficient to meet the needs of the human heart, I have

come to feel a renewed love for God. I realize He has gently taken me through so much. I still do not understand so many things, but have learned what *hope* is—another piece of the complex puzzle God has tried to show me these months.

For years I have been the eternal optimist. Now I understand that eternal optimism can be a denial of reality. It is not hope.

Julie has had to face the reality that the debt she and her husband hold of more than $125,000 may take a lifetime to remove, her husband's spiritual life may be stagnant forever, their relationship is for all practical purposes dead—her feelings for him numb except for resentment or bitterness at the situation he initiated, causing them to lose almost everything—she has hit a brick wall.

And Bill, Carol's husband, recently realized he may never marry again. Carol is dead, responsibilities for his children and ailing mother are both permanent and overwhelming. Bill hit a brick wall. Like Julie and Bill, I realize reality means that life may never be as it was. Life events as they have unfolded may never change. Something died inside at this truth. I hit a brick wall.

In the face of stark despairing reality, I realize we lose "optimism." Optimism always looks for human possibilities and solutions to solve problems. The proverbial "card up the sleeve" disappears. At this point when denial is removed and reality strikes, *hope* is born.

What is hope? Hope recognizes the truth about a situation while choosing to focus on the supernatural reality of divine intervention. Not only does God become the focus, but the reality on which we depend. God and His ability to make impossible things possible anchors our hope. *He is God beyond the brick wall.* That's hope.

It's not a trust placed in what can be seen but in what cannot. "But hope that is seen is no hope at all," Paul writes in Romans.[6]

David expressed it this way, "Find rest, O my soul, in God alone; my hope comes from him."[7]

Promise after promise is offered in the Bible so that we might have hope; and they are God's promises of love. Here are more.

"But the eyes of the Lord are on those who fear him, on those whose hope is in his unfailing love."[8]

"No one whose hope is *in you* will ever be put to shame."[9]

The Master Designer gives us courage to go on because our hope is active, not passive. It is something we can do as we trust and wait. "Be joyful in hope, patient in affliction, faithful in prayer."[10] Paul adds, "May the God of hope fill you with all joy and peace as you trust in him, so that you may overflow with hope by the power of the Holy Spirit."[11]

And the doing—the hopeful believing—*is* faith, "Now faith is being sure of what we hope for and certain of what we do not see."[12]

God, whose power extends beyond the brick wall, helps me to respond as David, "Why are you downcast, O my soul? Why so disturbed within me? Put your hope in God, for I will yet praise him, my Savior and my God."[13]

The Faces of Blindness

Whether it's misplaced optimism or complete denial of truth, blindness fails to manage the chaos in our life, just as structuring does. The Chaos Factor persists. If your answers to the test in chapter 2 indicated that blindness is your preferred coping mechanism, you need to realize this: blindness doesn't make the chaos go away.

Those of us who use blindness techniques do not generally see things to be as bad as they are. We create our own picture of the chaotic situation and ignore anything that attempts to threaten our picture.

For example, even though Dad seems continually depressed, we simply choose to believe he's having a bad day. The situation is probably much more serious than we're willing to admit. Or the fact that Tommy is consistently receiving D grades proves he's struggling academically, but we blame the teacher. We're certain she's simply inept.

Many of those who choose blindness operate by a philosophy something like this: Every unhappy event in life has a beginning, middle, and end; if we can just get to the end, we'll survive, so we can ignore the middle and eventually it will end. Blindness seldom looks back. It doesn't assess past difficulties but denies them. As a result, the same difficulties pop up again and again. The person never learns from the past.

Chosen blindness offers only the illusion of safety, predictability, and control. It masks the truth and invites calamity. As you stand in the middle of the highway, you can tell yourself that the huge truck bearing down on you doesn't really exist and everything will be fine. But ultimately the truth will prevail. If you don't get out of the way, you will encounter the truck, and it won't be fun.

When we choose blindness, we cherish illusions rather than truth in an effort to find closure. Rather than confronting our chaos with God, we simply want the chaos to end.

This bleak picture is not uncommon. We all use blindness as a system for responding to chaos. Psychotherapist E. Devers Braden, quoted by Alice Kosner in "Making the Best of Change," attests to this: "The majority of people walk around in a trance ninety percent of the time—live their lives on automatic. So there's tremendous anxiety about becoming conscious. When coping with the world, you have to be aware of every action you take. It's like driving a car—turning the ignition key, looking in a rearview mirror, backing out of the parking space, signaling for a turn, watching out for other cars on the freeway. It's excruciating."[14]

Kosner concludes, "Still, unconsciousness may be even more painful, especially when you have to handle unexpected—or unwanted—change."[15] Blindness leaves you unprepared for a healthy response to the chaos of life.

But we all seem to rely on it to some extent. We see this even in biblical characters. Isaac chose to believe his son Jacob when he posed as his elder brother Esau to gain the blessing. Yes, Isaac was physically blind, but he still had several clues about Jacob's real identity. Yet he chose to ignore those warning signals—why would his family resort to trickery? And so, Isaac blinded himself to reality.[16] What about those who scorned Noah's warning of a calamitous flood? They watched Noah build an ark, heard his invitations, and danced to their death in chosen blindness.[17]

The Ultimate Act of Blindness

We see resistance through blindness most dramatically in the account of Jesus' crucifixion and resurrection. Jesus was crucified. Removed from the cross, he was placed in a tomb and guarded by Roman soldiers. "Early on Sunday morning, as the new day was dawning, Mary Magdalene and the other Mary went out to see the tomb. Suddenly there was a great earthquake, because an angel of the Lord came down from heaven and rolled aside the stone and sat on it. His face shone like lightning, and his clothing was as white as snow. The guards shook with fear when they saw him, and they fell into a dead faint."

As the women hurried into the city to tell others, some of the guards went to the leading priests and told them what had happened. A meeting of the religious leaders was called to deal with this chaotic situation. They decided to bribe the soldiers, with the orders: "You must say, 'Jesus' disciples came during the night while we were sleeping, and they stole the body.'"

In other words, you only *think* you saw an angel in front of an empty tomb. From this day forth, as far as you're concerned, the disciples stole the body, and that's the way it is. Blind yourself to the truth and create a fabrication that will become the truth to which all will adhere.

"So the guards accepted the bribe and said what they were told to say. Their story spread widely among the Jews, and they still tell it today."[18]

Blindness, blatant or subtle, temporarily seems to conquer the chaos. But it also shuts out the truth and keeps you from dealing honestly with God.

Spiritualizing the Chaos

You know Evelyn, or someone like her. The last time you were in a personal or family crisis, she was there—armed with her smile and a Bible. Maybe you were mourning the death of a loved one. Well, Evelyn caught you in your vulnerable moment and spent the next two hours telling you why you should be happy, not sad. The dearly departed is free of pain; no more suffering. You should be happy he's in heaven. Happy you'll be with him again someday.

Awkward and uncomfortable with the pain of your loss, Evelyn lives in a world of blindness and tries to draw you into it—and she even uses the Bible to do so. She refuses to acknowledge pain, and expects you to refuse it, too. But she's not doing you any favors. She's merely turning a blind eye to God's truth.

Carol, my friend who died of cancer, commented on the Evelyns in her life, those who visited with good intentions and chronic blindness. Their favorite Bible verse was always Romans 8:28, "God causes all things to work together for good to those who love God, to those who are called according to His purpose." Carol always remarked, "But they forget to notice the verse that follows, Romans 8:29, that we might 'become conformed to the image of His Son.'" God will do anything necessary to accomplish this purpose and it's rarely easy or comfortable to experience the radical internal changes implicit in this transformation.

Abandoning Our Defenses and Devices

Don't be too hard on Nancy, Josh, Angie, or even Evelyn. Remember that we all implement one or more of these strategies of structure or blindness. Some of us are very good at both.

But all our strategies serve us only as long as the illusion of their security persists. When all our abilities to manage chaos fail us, God is there. Our world doesn't fall apart, even if our feelings are crying, "Mayday!" Because God holds us. We rest secure in his grasp, cared for and loved. He promises, "I have loved you with an everlasting love,"[19] and "The eternal God is your refuge and underneath are the everlasting arms."[20]

As you recognize the faulty coping mechanisms you've employed to manage the chaos in your life, you will come face to face with God. And as you surrender these protective devices, he will give you a gift beyond description—the gift of himself. God fills these empty places with his presence and provides a comfort and security that never fails. Lovingly he teaches a new way of seeing, a new way of living.

We have taken the first two steps to rest, the first two steps in the Chaos Factor.

Step 1: Acknowledge that chaos is the raw material of life.

Step 2: Recognize your responses of resistance to chaos and face the truth.

The next step in our journey goes beyond recognizing our self-designed chaos management systems that replace God. Step 3 is to abandon your faulty systems for chaos management.

Step 3: Abandon your faulty systems for chaos management.

Why? Because they're idols.

Idols? Yes, idols. We don't use that word much anymore, do we? Immediately our mind pictures wooden carvings, incense, and worshiped statues. But an idol is anything that replaces God in our life, anything we love more than we love the Divine Conductor of chaos.

When I've spoken of idols in the past, I've described them as things, whether golf clubs, wardrobe, sports car, home decor according to *House Beautiful,* job promotion, or our children's accomplishments.

But my understanding of idolatry has since expanded, based on a new grasp of the relationship God desires with us. Two statements in the Bible speak of the all-consuming love God has for us:

"Do not worship any other god, for the LORD, whose name is Jealous, is a jealous God."[21]

"For the LORD your God is a consuming fire, a jealous God."[22]

Henri Nouwen writes,

God is a lover who does not want to leave us alone for one second of our day or night. God is asking for our total, undivided attention.... He wants us to love him through thanksgiving, praise, intercession, and service at all times and places, unceasingly, with every fiber of our being. Indeed, God is a very, very jealous lover.

We didn't choose him. He chose us (John 15:16). We may be interested in some of his attention at certain times, but he offers us all his attention at all times, whether we are interested or not. He does not give us much leeway. No, he wants us here, now, totally, and unconditionally.

Yes, God is a jealous God, but God's jealousy is not filled with possessiveness and suspicion, as is our human jealousy. There is not a tinge of hatred, resentment, or revenge in God. God loves us with a perfect love, a love that casts out all fear and allows us to approach God and his people in complete freedom.[23]

Have you ever thought of God as a jealous lover? Have you given much thought to the Divine Conductor who orchestrates chaos, creation, and your life as well? His love is so great that he refuses to allow anything to compete for your returned affection. He wants intimacy with you, and he tolerates nothing that separates you from him.

Do I sound melodramatic, describing God as a jealous lover? I didn't make this up. Scripture shouts it, in the verses I've quoted and in many other passages (see the Book of Hosea, for instance). The truth is that your love matters to God. He takes it very seriously. You matter to God—and he wants nothing less than his best for you.

This is not a passive issue. It remains, throughout all history, the pivotal issue of human existence. God offers his love. Will we accept and respond to it? Our question is not, Where is God when it hurts? Our question is, Are we with God when it hurts? Are we running to him or into the arms of another lover?

Our Idolatrous Coping Mechanisms

For some, when chaos hits, their blindness system promises refuge in the arms of a person other than their spouse. Of course, this results in broken relationships and incomprehensible pain. Such relationships become idolatry—a replacement for security in God.

Others run to the movies in response to chaos. Long ago, entertainment became the opium of the people. Movie stars and athletes have become heroes to be worshiped. The impact of the entertainment field has changed the way we see the world—news is no longer information but entertainment. We often talk about individual stars as idols, but the truth is that the entire experience of entertainment can become an idol.

Still others, when chaos strikes, run to the refrigerator. Food is their idol. Witness the growing number of weight-loss programs. In a *U.S. News and World Report* article titled "A Godly Approach to Weight Loss" we read, "Most people don't associate religious devotion with weight loss. Gwen Shamblin, a Tennessee dietitian, does. She's the author of the new book, *The Weigh Down,* which teaches that 'head hunger,' the urge to eat even when the body doesn't need food, is really a 'spiritual hunger.' Weight loss the Shamblin way is a matter of 'substituting God for food.'" The reporter continues by describing other religious programs for weight loss and then concludes, "Their approaches differ, but their message is the same: Transfer that love of food to a love of God."[24]

Amid chaos, other people attempt to find security in their careers, drowning themselves in busyness. Or in money, striving to accumulate enough to feel secure. Or in the control that comes through personal achievement and the praise of others.

For some, the idol is intellectual pursuit. If they can analyze and understand, they're in control. Others seek security in self-gratification. Hoping that pleasure will replace misery, they skydive, motorcycle, horseback ride, or participate in the latest craze.

We really depend on these mechanisms, don't we? It's hard to admit, but we've grown to love them. They make us feel secure, protected, safe. If the truth were known, we would rather die than abandon them, because deep inside we believe we will die without them.

God in the Midst of Chaos

We know God is in the midst of our chaos. We know he wants us to trust him. But we may fear that he won't come through for us. Not *this* time, anyway. What if he's there for you but not for me? What if he's too busy, or I'm unworthy, or he doesn't really care?

That's it, isn't it? What if God doesn't really love you?

But he does. He says so. Just as he promised Jeremiah, he promises you, "I know the plans I have for you . . . plans to prosper you and not to harm you, plans to give you a hope and a future."[25] You can trust him. It's a process, tearing down the idols in your life and replacing them with trust and dependence on God. One step at a time. But one thing I can promise you: He is absolutely trustworthy. He never fails to come through.

Maybe not in the way you expected.

Maybe not on your timetable.

But he is there for you and will act on your behalf. It's his promise, and he is Truth. He cannot lie.

So will you venture into the turbulent waters of chaos? Will you let God show you the coping mechanisms that have kept you from him? Will you let go of those leaky lifesavers and trust God to buoy you?

To possess the new, we must abandon the old. And it's amazing how hard it is to give up those idols, even though we know they're faulty and unsatisfactory. As psychotherapist E. Devers Braden writes, "Trying something new means giving up our old ways, our old patterns and modes of functioning. This leads to a fear of the unknown. We're afraid we're going to leave our old life behind."[26]

But that's exactly what I'm challenging you to do. When you let go of your idols, you open the door to a new experience with God. You might consider voicing these words I've said so often: "Lord, show me my idols. Give me courage to face them and begin the arduous task of abandoning them and the security they deceitfully promise. May I place my trust in you and you alone.

"The next time chaos strikes and I am tempted to run to my idols, I will pray the words of Lamentations, 'Because of the LORD'S great love we are not consumed, for his compassions never fail. They are new every morning; great is your faithfulness,' and I will remember, 'The LORD is my portion; therefore I will wait for him.'[27] Your all-sufficiency is my place of hope and rest."

If you have not yet taken the first Chaos Factor steps, choose to now. Move three steps closer to hope in the midst of chaos.

Step 1: Acknowledge that chaos is the raw material of life.
Step 2: Recognize your responses of resistance to chaos and face the truth.
Step 3: Abandon your faulty systems for chaos management.

Abandoning old systems is not comfortable. You will experience a sense of loss and grief. But on the other side of the grief is a hope beyond anything imagined. In the next chapter we will take the final difficult step before developing healthy responses to chaos which promise peace and hope.

A Step into Sorrow

> Anesthesia, which is most useful on occasions of surgery, is most harmful in matters of the soul.
>
> Eugene H. Peterson

I slip out as quickly as possible, looking up to admire the fall foliage and breathe the musky air. I heave a sigh of relief. It's been a year now since Carol's death. Little has changed; the pain persists. I walk the brick path from my friend's home to my car. Inside, others continue to chatter and chuckle, exchanging the pleasantries of conversation. But I want out. Forced to express a cheerfulness I don't feel, I retreat. After expressing my sincere thank yous, I excuse myself.

On the path, I relax, glad to be fleeing social demands. I hear fallen leaves crunching behind me, and I snap to attention. I'm being followed. I quicken my pace, but the footsteps behind me quicken, too. As I reach my car door, I hear my name. Caught!

"Linda, are you okay?" asks my friend Pam. "I'm sorry you have to leave early. Is everything all right?"

Reluctantly, I smile. "I've got some errands to run. I'll be okay."

She notices my reticence, sees that everything is not okay, and decides to continue the conversation. "I came after you because there's something I've been wanting to tell you for a long time. You know that course you've been teaching on relationships? I really appreciate your vulnerability. I know losing Carol was really painful for you. But I want you to know how much your admitting your pain has really meant to all of us. You seem *real* for the first time."

She looked away for a moment, seeming to choose her words carefully. "Always before you seemed so cheerful about *everything*. It made us feel like you lived on some plane six feet above us all—a plane *we'd* never reach. I'd always held the mistaken idea you described, the mistaken belief that really 'spiritual' Christians must have a plastered smile across their faces all the time or else something is wrong with them. I thought if something hurt me or if I admitted life wasn't okay, I simply didn't have enough faith."

I was stunned by her words. She went on.

"It was like Christianity couldn't be lived in the real world. I thought I had to create an unreal world for Christianity to survive. Now I know that's not true. Your words, 'Jesus never said life was easy; he simply said he'd be there no matter what,' have really changed my life."

She smiled and placed in my hand a photocopy of a pen-and-ink drawing. "Here. I found a picture I wanted you to have. Thanks again for being real. I'll be praying for you." She started to leave, but turned back. "Thanks again."

"Thanks, Pam," I said, staring down at the picture in my hand. A little boy sat huddled in a tree on the top of a dark mountain. He looked troubled and sad. The inscription beneath the picture read, "So I stayed on my lofty height, lonely and proud and cold."

A Step into Sorrow

I've thought about that encounter with Pam many times since. Before she verbalized her thoughts, I hadn't realized how often my appearance denied the deeper realities of my life. I'd always considered myself the eternal optimist—and that was a good thing. When life gave me lemons, I made lemonade; that was how I coped with pain. Much of my life was spent in denial.

Pam was right. I had been living on some "superspiritual" plane, where I refused to admit the pain I felt. Even as I express this, my memory flashes to a moment when I was only six or eight, headed for the doctor's office, terrified about getting a shot. My aunt gave me a bit of advice: "If the doctor gives you a shot, just close your eyes, turn your head away, and think about something else while you hum a tune."

I took her advice, and it worked. I never even felt the needle. And that became my method for dealing with all the pain in my life. If I didn't look, it couldn't hurt me. If I didn't see, it couldn't touch me. I pursued a pain-free life.

Isn't that the all-American dream? Life without pain. We spend our lifetimes trying to attain it. If we can only amass enough wealth, buy enough things, gain enough recognition, take enough pills, or reach enough goals, we'll have that pain-free life of our dreams. Television commercials trumpet this message, offering medicine for every ache or sniffle. Sweepstakes contests bank on it. "When our prize crew arrives at your door, your problems are over," they promise.

But a pain-free life is not real life. Nor is it a goal worthy of our aspiration. Not only is it impossible, but to be free of pain would remove the possibility of transformation—positive change that produces good. Before positive change takes place, we must feel that something isn't right, that there's some problem that creates a need to change. We recognize problems through the pain we experience. If life were pain-free, we'd never see the need to change. We'd never grow. We'd become self-satisfied, proud. And pride isolates us, leaving us like the little boy in the picture—lonely and cold. Pain reminds us that we live in a broken world with hope and the possibility of improvement.

The Pain of Idolatry

In the last chapter, we considered the personal idolatry most of us maintain, a dependence on something other than God in the midst of chaos. Step 3 for dealing with chaos (abandon your faulty systems for chaos management) recognizes that we must depose these idols before we can fully trust God and learn his ways of responding to chaos.

Abandoning our idols is imperative, but isn't it difficult? We've clung to them all our lives. Giving them up hurts, even though these coping mechanisms are faulty and sure to disappoint.

We see this struggle in the life of Israel, God's chosen nation. The entire Bible is the story of God's loving pursuit of his people, and their constant refusal to love and trust only him. He would woo them with signs and wonders, making promises to bless and enrich them, promises he faithfully kept. As a result, the people would draw near, choosing to trust God, and he would bless them abundantly. But time and again, they would turn away and choose their own way, depending on their own or other human resources to protect and provide for them. This was dramatically demonstrated when Israel asked the prophet Samuel for a king.

Samuel had served as priest and ruling judge for many years, but he was getting old and his sons were unqualified to succeed him. The elders of Israel wanted security for the future. All the other nations had kings; Israel wanted a king, too. This disturbed Samuel, so he decided to discuss it with God in prayer. God's response was, "Listen to all that the people are saying to you; it is not you they have rejected, but they have rejected me as their king. As they have done from the day I brought them up out of Egypt until this day, forsaking me and serving other gods, so they are doing to you."[1] They wanted a king to replace God, the rightful and only king of Israel.

Why? Because they wanted to be like everybody else. They wanted a ruler they could see and follow, a flesh-and-blood leader.

God outlined the detrimental consequences of this choice. He told them a human king would make their sons and daughters slaves to run in front of *his* chariots, commanders at war to lead and die before *his* armies, laborers in *his* fields. He would take the crops they grow and give them to *his* attendants. He would demand a tenth of all they had to give to *his* staff. He would take the best of their families, their servants, and their animals for *his* property. And if they chose this path, God added, he would not respond when they cried out for relief from this king they demanded.

Samuel repeated God's words and asked the people to reconsider. They insisted, "'No! We want a king over us. Then we will be like all the other nations, with a king to lead us and to go out before us and fight our battles.' . . . The LORD answered, 'Listen to them and give them a king.'"[2]

They were choosing blindness, ignoring the problems that God was predicting. They were clinging to the idol of monarchy. Who cared what God said? Their king would save them.

The resulting heartache extends to this day. Whenever people decide that the Divine Orchestrator of life is not enough for them, the results are devastating. And we suffer the consequences until we turn from our own way to his, giving up our idols and clinging to him.

The Pain of Removing Our Idols

There are three types of pain in this process: disillusionment, grieving over the loss of our old patterns, and the personal sorrow of repentance.

1. The Sorrow of Disillusionment

First, we face the pain of disillusionment, accepting the fact that we live in a broken world, that life simply will never work as we would hope. Our lives will never be perfect.

This may seem a simple truth, but it's one we ardently resist. We have great expectations. We think we deserve certain things. One may believe she has a right to a wonderful marriage in which her husband adores and "loves her as Christ loves his church." Another may believe he deserves a successful career with the dividends of admiration, monetary reward, and prestige.

But the truth is that, in an imperfect world, life rarely meets our expectations. Neither life nor God owes us anything. That can be a painful thing to realize, but until we do, we can't respond to chaos effectively.

One psychotherapist explains, "People have a dream, and they believe that if the dream is fulfilled, life will be perfect—they'll no longer have any problems. The disparity between expectations and reality often sets off a 'postpartum depression.'"[3] An interesting term. Postpartum depression occurs as a mother mourns the separation of her baby from her body. In the same way, we cherish our false dreams as we carry them within us. It's hard to deliver them into the harsh light of reality.

Passionately, Saint Augustine says it best. "Here is the naked truth: My human soul shrinks in horror from laying down my rights, wants, compulsions, demands. What if, in humbling myself, I'm set aside and forgotten? What if my wants are left hungering?"[4] That is the root of our sorrow. We fear that if we abandon our false expectations for life, God will not be enough for us.

Tammy was planning to get married to a wonderful Christian man God had brought into her life. The wedding plans were well under way, and they were about to send out the invitations when her fiancé dropped a bombshell—he had been visiting prostitutes for the previous ten years. Shocked, Tammy insisted that they enter counseling before the wedding plans went any further. But in the counselor's office, the situation got worse. Her fiancé said he never loved her and really didn't want to marry her.

Tammy was left alone. She'd lost the person closest to her. She felt God had left her, too. Oh, she knew mentally that God was still there, but she sure felt betrayed by him. This was an ongoing struggle for her. She felt like Job, sitting alone amid the ashes.

"I had to stop and feel my emotions, instead of denying things happened," she said later, reliving those painful days. "I brought my emotions to God, as raw as they were. I knew he could take it.

"I know God is ultimately in control. I know God is all-powerful and always faithful. I know I'm not alone. He will always be with me. My journey is finding my way back to him."

One of God's names is El Shaddai. Though its meaning is uncertain, "God is the rock or mountain" appears to be the best rendering and is translated Almighty God. What does this mean? Almighty points to God's sufficiency. We can allow ourselves to experience the pain of disillusionment and then embrace the truth because God will be there. He will be enough.

God also invites us to lament over our unrealized expectations. The Psalms and Job both give us permission to struggle with God. Struggling is painful. David cries out to God, "How long, O LORD? Will you forget me forever? How long will you hide your face from me? How long must I wrestle with my thoughts and every day have sorrow in my heart?"[5]

Job is willing to confront God with the things that simply don't add up. They appear inconsistent with his understanding of God. But God isn't disturbed by Job's questioning. As a matter of fact, God is more disturbed by Job's friends who offer pat answers that deny Job's struggle. God condemns Job's friends, "You have not spoken of [God] what is right."[6]

In his distress, Job removed any spiritual clichés and said exactly what he thought about God. On the other hand, his friends' words were laced with pretense, arrogance, pride, and well-worn truisms. Counselor Don Allender writes, "Behind spiritual pretense that has no room for honest struggle with God is the assumption that trust precludes struggle; faith erases doubt; hope removes despair."[7]

Another counselor, Judy Stewart, concludes, "In our attempts to make sure not only we, but God, come off looking spiritual, we sing with placid smiles, quote scriptures with correct tonal emphasis, nod our heads and say 'amen' at the right times, polish our attendance buttons, and live life with little conviction that the gospel makes any significant difference. Trust, love, and obedience are reduced to an external behavioral system rather than significant elements in our relationship with the mysterious, wondrous God of the universe. When we refuse to lament, we declare God impotent and defraud ourselves and God of true worship."[8]

Only when we honestly lament the inconsistencies between our expectations and reality can we enter the struggle with God without pretense. To lament is to refuse to close our hearts to God, to rage against the temporary grip of the grim reaper, master of a sinful dying world. Stewart adds, "Lament is a willingness to enter a time of darkness, giving full vent to our pain and allowing our thoughts about God to flow honestly."[9]

When her marriage crumbled into divorce, Gay was afraid to allow herself to grieve over lost hopes and dreams, so she emotionally steeled herself in an attempt to survive. Years later, she realized that she had succeeded so well in stifling her pain that she felt emotionally numb. She no longer knew how to feel. She felt no pain, but felt no joy, either. She felt nothing. As time passed, she wanted to feel again but didn't know where to begin.

"I realized I had to stop running from pain," she explained later. "I had to convince myself that, if I allowed myself to feel it, I wouldn't be destroyed. After the divorce, it seemed any pain was too much—more than I could handle. Yet I had survived the divorce and had handled it, so I didn't need to fear it any longer."

Though Gay lives in a cold climate, she hates the cold and escapes it whenever possible. But that winter, she used the cold to teach herself something about pain. Rather than fleeing the cold at a moment's notice, sometimes she would stand outside, allowing the cold to penetrate her coat to her skin, even to her bones.

"I would allow myself to feel the cold and realize it held no power over me," she explains. "I could go inside any time I chose.

A Step into Sorrow

I didn't have to be afraid of the cold anymore. I used this to prove to myself that I could let myself feel pain in the same way. I could stop the process whenever I chose, so I didn't need to descend into despair or depression. I didn't have to be afraid of the pain anymore. It wouldn't destroy me. That may seem silly, but it worked."

And as she allowed herself to feel pain, she opened herself to other emotions as well. She was no longer afraid to feel.

Psychologist Stephen Gullo remarks, "More traumatic, perhaps, than being laid off or fired can be the breakup of a relationship. In extreme cases, an individual can experience loveshock, a state of psychological numbness, disorientation and emptiness."[10] Like Gay, we can overcome the numbness through our willingness to acknowledge our pain—*by choosing to feel it.*

We began this chapter with Eugene Peterson's quote, "Anesthesia, which is most useful on occasions of surgery, is most harmful in matters of the soul."[11] Growing numb and anesthetized is not healthy for the soul. We must choose to feel our pain.

One spring, Marty learned that her fourteen-year-old daughter had Hodgkin's disease. It was the biggest crisis any member of her family had ever faced, but they faced it with faith. God seemed very close to them all as young Corina went through chemotherapy, hair loss, and then, joyously, remission.

But two years later, the girl had a recurrence of the problem and needed further treatment. The calm acceptance Marty had shown the first time around was nowhere to be found. "Why, God, does she have to go through this again?" she cried. "Lord, why does this have to happen in her senior year? What lessons did we not learn, that we must face chemo again, this time more of it, and with stronger medicines? Hasn't she already been tried in the fire and come out as purified gold?" It didn't seem fair.

The chaos of numerous doctors' visits and treatments didn't help any. Some required a four-hour round trip. Tears and agonized questions flowed freely. Marty also struggled to balance her time with Corina's two younger siblings, helping them share their own fears.

In the midst of all this, Marty was asked to start a morning Bible study at her church. If anyone had an excuse to beg out of this project, Marty did, but she knew that no one else would get it done. "I needed the study more than anyone. It was imperative for me to show God's sufficiency in giving me the strength to start this," she explains.

So she did. And God blessed her efforts. Rather than drawing energy away from Marty's family crisis, the Bible study group proved a source of support. Group members did all they could to help. Other women took leadership when Marty couldn't, but God enabled Marty to be there often. "One reason the study is so important for me," she says, "is that it keeps me immersed in the living water of God's Word. Without that focus, I quickly sink. It may seem trite, but as long as my focus is the Lord Jesus, I keep from panicking. When I look at the waves around me, I feel myself sinking. But I'm so glad to have the foundation of belief that permits me to cry out, 'Jesus, save me,' when I feel helpless."

At this point, Marty doesn't know how Corina's treatments will turn out. Now the girl faces a stem-cell transplant, during which she is given "lethal doses" of chemotherapy. That's very frightening, but without it they'd live in fear of more recurrences.

Corina's faith has grown, and so has Marty's. For the first time in Marty's twenty-year marriage, she and her husband are attempting to pray together each morning. A strong, self-sufficient type, Marty's husband never needs help from anyone—but he's beginning to acknowledge his daily need for God, even though he has been a Christian for twenty-five years. In fact, Marty's whole church has developed a new closeness and a fresh commitment to prayer.

"Even if God should take Corina to heaven to be with him and my heart would be wrenched," Marty says, "I know he is sovereign. He walks through the fire with men, and I will not be burned."[12]

Marty has learned that when disillusionment and despair threaten to overtake her, God offers a supernatural peace beyond description. We, too, can rest in that knowledge. God wants us to express our disillusionment and despair to him, because he is able to help. The pain is real, and God operates in the real world to heal and support us. But you can't solve a problem that doesn't exist, and you can't help a person who refuses to acknowledge a need.

2. *The Sorrow of Loss*

A second pain that comes with idol-smashing is simply the sorrow of loss. Our systems of chaos management so permeate our lives that we grow to cherish them. The sorrow of losing them may feel overwhelming. Busyness, schedules, and meeting demands provide an addictive, artificial adrenaline high. New medical research proves that in our society this high becomes so routine that to relax and live at a normal, healthy pace is frightening. Many have attempted to get out of the rat race only to return after a few weeks or months.

Others sell their souls to careers, which become their idols. Enormous amounts of time, energy, cherishing, and nurturing are sacrificial offerings to the objects of worship. Blindness mechanisms keep the worshipers from realizing the cost: loss of marriage, of family, of real relationships forfeited for the artificial, temporary substitute of career success. If a careerist is ever downsized out of a job, is demoted, or gives up the career to follow God more fully—that sense of loss is profound.

A friend of mine held a top management position, supervising more than fifty employees. Due to the long hours and tedious demands, her health failed. After being hospitalized for several weeks to recuperate from pericarditis (an inflammation of the lining of the heart), she returned to her job. She discovered that all her responsibilities had been reassigned. Work had continued, and it seemed she had hardly been missed. She resigned that day. Since then, she has often repeated the lesson she learned: "Don't ever forget—no one is indispensable. Leave the workplace, and you are quickly forgotten. The only place you may be irreplaceable is in your family."

Whatever our idols, it is painful to give them up because we love them. The truth is we love them more than we love God, and it's time to place him as king on his rightful throne in our hearts. It is time to experience the sorrow of loss and move forward.

The great artist Michelangelo made an amazing statement before his death. "So now from this mad passion which made me take Art for an idol and a king, I have learnt the burden of error that it bore and what misfortunes spring from man's desire. The world's frivolities have robbed me of the time that I was given for reflecting upon God."

3. The Sorrow of Repentance

The third pain, following disillusionment and loss, is the pain of repentance. Repentance means turning away from something permanently. It involves an admission that you're heading the wrong way and a commitment to make a complete turnaround. In that process, a person realizes how much he or she has missed by trusting false coping mechanisms rather than God. And that's painful to think about.

In the New Testament, James describes it like this, "Come near to God and he will come near to you. Wash your hands, you sinners, and purify your hearts, you double-minded. Grieve, mourn and wail. Change your laughter to mourning and your joy to gloom. Humble yourselves before the Lord, and he will lift you up."[13]

One member of the Puritan group understood this concept well. He wrote this prayer:

> When thou wouldst guide me
>   I control myself.
> When thou wouldst be sovereign
>   I rule myself.
> When thou wouldst take care of me
>   I suffice myself.
> When I should depend on thy providings
>   I supply myself.
> When I should submit to thy providence
>   I follow my will.

A Step into Sorrow

> When I should study, honour, trust thee,
>   I serve myself.
> I fault and correct thy laws
>   to suit myself.
> Instead of thee I look to man's approbation,
>   and am by nature an idolater.
> Lord, it is my chief design to bring my heart back to
>   Thee.[14]

Yet the greatest sorrow is this. Jesus paid the penalty for our rebellion against God. He suffered for our idol worship. Prisoners sentenced to death die for their crimes, but Jesus died for *ours*.

It is right for us to mourn the fact that Jesus had to die because of our ruthless stubbornness. If we refuse to mourn, we scoff at Jesus' sacrifice.

God says, "They will look on me, the one they have pierced, and they will mourn for him as one mourns for an only child, and grieve bitterly for him as one grieves for a firstborn son.... On that day a fountain will be opened ... to cleanse them from sin and impurity. On that day, I will banish the names of the idols from the land, and they will be remembered no more."[15]

When we choose to mourn over our idolatry, God will assert his mighty power to eliminate our idols for us, but he'll comfort us as well, proving all-sufficient for our every need.

The Bible often refers to mourning. It's a natural part of the rhythm of life, though modern Americans seem to know little about it. The words to the song "Turn, Turn, Turn" that rippled from every teenager's radio in the 1960s arise from a biblical text that describes this rhythm. "There is a time for everything, and a season for every activity under heaven ... a time to weep and a time to laugh, a time to mourn and a time to dance."[16] Mourning is a cleansing, life-giving process that offers an opportunity to move freely into the future.

The Bible teaches that Jesus came to the earth "to comfort all who mourn,"[17] and God's promise is "I will turn their mourning into gladness; I will give them comfort and joy instead of sorrow."[18]

Sorrow enables us to turn from the false paradigms that have ordered our lives and frees us to choose new, effective patterns for our thinking and actions.

Continuing the Journey

Reading this book, you may already be changing your paradigms for life. We have seen that, contrary to popular belief, chaos is the raw material of life, permeating every aspect of our existence. Our attempts to resist it by blindness, ignoring it, elimination, management, and control are worthless—a fool's pursuit. The challenge is to risk the pain of sorrow and abandon our self-created, faulty systems, exchanging them for a dependence on the God of the universe. In the process, we discover peace as life's ebb and flow weaves our chaos into a divine tapestry, promising a good result in its finished design.

Now, as we have taken these steps or at least begun the process of acknowledging the chaos and recognizing we can respond differently, we are able to learn practical, hands-on ways to prepare for and respond to life's chaos—ways that embrace it rather than resist it. With these tools, we will find rest for our souls.

Part 2

Embracing the Chaos

Finding Peace in the Process

> Life is a continuous process of living and learning, longing and losing, with loving and laughing filling the gaps in between.
>
> Unknown

***Instant** coffee* . . . instant credit . . . instant information. Ours is an instant society. Our insatiable desire for instant gratification shapes our thinking. We expect instant solutions to our problems, instant answers to life's perplexities.

But guess what? It's all a lie. And that's what our next step is about—getting past the false hope of instant solutions and learning to accept the slow, steady *processes* of life.

Beginning with Step 1, we acknowledged that chaos is the raw material of life. In Step 2 we realized our tendency to resist the chaos, examining the coping mechanisms we use. Step 3 urged us to reject these coping methods, though that might be difficult. The next step prepares us to meet God in the chaos. Step 4 is to discover peace in life's process.

Step 4: Discover peace in life's process.

I recently read this description of inner peace:

It's not something you can order in, like pizza supreme. Inner peace happens to you in small, but extraordinary, moments. Like when you find two matching socks in the dryer. Or when the checkbook balances.

Or when you've just had your oil changed. Inner peace is a kind of silence within—within the bathroom, within the car, within the hall closet—anywhere you can hide.

No one under the age of thirty has inner peace.

After that, it can come over you at any time, like hiccups or *déjà vu*.

Inner peace is as elusive as an ATM passcode . . .

as mysterious as the buttons on a VCR . . .

as normal as peanut butter.

Don't worry about getting it. And you'll get it.

We chuckle at this crude definition of inner peace, but is this a description of peace at all . . . elusive, momentary, undependable? I don't think so.

True peace is found in a life dependent on God. It comes through a relationship with his Son. And it's constant. When we rely on the fact that God knows what he's doing, has the power to do it, and is accomplishing it even now as we live, we find peace. There is peace in the process of life.

Jesus assures us, "I have told you these things, so that in me you may have peace. In this world you will have trouble. But take heart! I have overcome the world."[1] Eugene Peterson rephrases Jesus' words in language we may more easily apply: "The Father is with me. I've told you all this so that trusting me, you will be unshakable and assured, deeply at peace. In this godless world you will continue to experience difficulties. But take heart! I've conquered the world."[2]

We've discussed our need to acknowledge our coping mechanisms. Now we can begin the process of removing them through faith in God. You can't overcome or even identify all of these faulty methods overnight, or in months, or even years. Identifying and then actually turning away from them is a lifelong process—and that's tough to accept in the instant society in which we live.

But we find great freedom in merely recognizing that it will take time. The pressure's off. You don't have to be an overnight success. You can take deliberate, steady steps.

Remember the Butterfly Effect from the first chapter? Meteorologist Edward Lorenz discovered that life isn't as ordered and predictable as it appears. But even more important, he stumbled on the amazing and energizing fact that the smallest changes can make profound differences. Even the smallest decisions we make and actions we take can produce positive change in our lives and the lives of others.

The Tyranny of Logic

I was raised to believe that every question has an answer, every problem a solution—if one simply reasons and considers it long enough (a few hours or perhaps days). Most Americans seem to think this. Our educational system is based on it. Aristotle started it, and science continued it.

Aristotle developed the structure of propositions and examination we now call logic. His philosophy determined logic to be fundamental to all life. Science seemed to confirm it, establishing the axiom that the mechanism of cause and effect is a requirement for scientific explanation. This is determinism.

What does this have to do with us? Read what Paul Geisert and Lynda Futrell write about chaos theory: "Science instruction led many of us through a physical world that was constructed of nice, clean, logical, linear systems. . . . We were told we could solve problems in logical fashion. Many of us generalized that concept to form a worldview that humans operate in a logical fashion. Did any of your science teachers tell you, 'That's not the way the world actually works'?"[3]

Excellent question. Mine didn't. How about yours? Life *isn't* logical. Answers rarely come quickly and sometimes don't come at all.

You probably realize this, but have you personalized it? Or do you still expect life to make sense if you find the right boxes to pack it into?

If life is basically chaotic, it can't be easily categorized. There's no instant, logical way to fix our problems in a broken world. The only way we'll find peace in this mess is to take the long view, to understand that life is a full and embracing process, not static or linear. All events, decisions, choices, mistakes, problems, and joys are woven into a rich fabric of this precious tapestry we call life. Nothing is wasted.

This is important because it redeems the past and offers hope for the future. Though you may grieve over mistakes and bad choices, all these blend to create a meaningful picture that constantly changes with new decisions and choices. Instead of looking for an instant solution the next time chaos strikes, you can accept chaos as part of the process. At the same time, you can make new choices that may significantly influence your future.

Denying the Process

Are you still trying to give your children all the "right" answers to their problems: specific, positively splendid directions for managing their lives? After all, that's your job as a parent, right? Not really.

Are you still attempting to change your spouse by offering all the "right" suggestions for success? If she'd simply do this or if he would do that, the problem would be solved. Each could move forward with a well-ordered life.

But life isn't like that. Problems may have many solutions. And the solutions may take months, or even years, to be realized.

I often vote for neat little boxes—sort of the divide and conquer approach. Simple, distinct, to the point. You have a problem. You find a solution. The goal—to institute the actions necessary to realize this solution. Problem solved. Issue closed. Ah . . . you sigh in deep relief. Job well done. Life can go on.

But life simply doesn't work that way.

Geisert and Futrell continue, "A chaotic system is one in which a number of *nonlinear* functions interact deterministically in a manner such that the outcomes cannot be predicted by humans, even with massive computers."[4]

Chaos is not linear, predictable, or logical. As a result, neither is life. To use the term *deterministically* seems a contradiction, but it's not. God determines the unfolding results, even though human determinism fails.

The Big Board Game of Life

Believe it or not, I was in my gynecologist's office when I started thinking about this process of life. It was several years ago. The dreaded exam over, Pap smear taken, mammogram complete—my blond, thirty-something doctor sat down to chat. Strange, I thought. His brow furrowed. He looked really perplexed. Oh no, I thought. What's wrong with me? Cancer?

"Linda, I know you're a writer."

Yes, I thought. *So please get to the point. You don't have to break this to me gently. Tell me what's wrong.*

"I've been wondering about something lately. You and I agree there is a God. If there *is* some rhyme or reason to this life, if God has a plan, then how do you explain the choices we make? Like the choice of one person for a mate over another? Or of one job or geographic location where we live over another? And how

Embracing the Chaos

do you figure in all the unexpected events of life? How can you say God has a plan or will if all these alter the picture and change the outcome daily? Then if there is a plan, can you miss it? Make the wrong choices, I mean?"

You could have knocked me over. I guess, as he saw it, being a writer made me the contemplative type. He must have assumed I'd have an answer to this series of questions. Well, I *am* the contemplative type, but this was not something I'd considered at the time. Or probably ever considered, to this extent anyway. Coming up with an immediate answer was quite a feat.

"Well . . ." I stalled. "I do believe there is a God. We definitely agree. And there is some plan to each life different from all others." Then I remembered a Bible verse I quoted earlier in this book. "It's sort of like God said to Jeremiah in the Bible, 'I know the plans I have for you. Plans for good and not for evil, to give you a future and a hope.'" I was glad I remembered it.

"God has a plan," I continued. "I guess I imagine that plan as a big board game. With birth, you begin at 'Go' and there are lots of different options. You make tons of choices. Some are good choices that affect your life for the good. Some are poor choices, and you sit out of the game for a while until you change the direction of your choices.

"When you acknowledge your mistake and make different choices, you get back in the game. Then even the mistake is mysteriously transformed into a benefit. For example, you learn something, or you make better choices the next time."

He grinned. "I'm sure glad to hear that. I've made enough bad choices to last a lifetime." We laughed.

"Sometimes good even comes out of the mistake," I added. "But the entire point is to make the best choices possible so you can fulfill the purpose you were born to fulfill."

He smiled in agreement and nodded for me to continue.

"Whatever your choices, they're woven into the fabric of your life. Throughout the process you are learning and growing. At the end of the game, you arrive at the predetermined conclusion, having fulfilled the purpose you were intended to, regardless of the path. The Divine Director brings order out of the orchestrated chaos to accomplish your best good."

"That sounds good to me," he said, smiling. "I've wondered about that. Any other thoughts?"

I reflected a moment and continued, "I guess the only exception would be if you sit out the whole game. Then you would be out of the will of God. That would happen as a result of bad choices which you continue to make. You simply miss the game plan. Though you are altogether aware you are making the wrong choices, you persist, unwilling to turn the corner to a new direction. Your life ends on some regrettable side road."

He nodded, understanding. We both grew silent for a moment. My mind flashed to the newspaper story I had read earlier. A well-known business chief executive officer, respected in his field and known for taking risks, made the fatal choice. Alcoholism got the best of him. Drunk, he died in an automobile accident on the way home from the bar.

"I can think of so many incidents where people make poor choices," I said. "The job is tough. They grow tired and angry at the demands. And in bitterness, they turn to some destructive behavior."

My doctor nodded. "I meet people like that in my office almost every week."

"In my mind," I said, "these are people who refuse to grow, learn, or change, who allow life events to control them, making them bitter instead of better. They opted out of the game of life years ago. They're cynical, angry, mean-spirited people moving toward death. That's their only goal."

I paused. His brow remained furrowed. "Then, what causes one choice to be good and another bad? On whose authority does good or bad hinge?"

"Well," I replied. "We're basing this discussion on the belief that God exists." I paused. "The Creator God has specific purposes for creating unique individuals with a different plan for each."

After another pause, I shrugged. "As I said, I've decided the Judeo-Christian faith is most consistent with life as I understand it. For me, the Bible is the instruction book of life given by a God who cares enough to help me live most beneficially. Only a cruel creator would leave us without direction or instruction for making good choices or forming accurate decisions. That's where the Bible comes in. There's got to be some outside standard for life—otherwise it would all be haphazard and meaningless. I feel it has been too intricately designed to be arbitrary or pointless."

Finally I understood his concern as a gynecologist specializing in cancer research who deals with cancer patients every day. He thoughtfully phrased his next question: "So then, when two people get cancer and one chooses treatment and lives while the other refuses it and dies, those choices simply become part of life's fabric and their purpose for living will still be realized?"

"I believe that," I said, remembering Carol, my friend who died of cancer. In her first bout with cancer, she had chosen all the treatments medical science could offer. Through the misery of chemotherapy, she had made that choice for the sake of her two sons. Would life have been different had she made a different choice? Probably. She wanted to be there for the boys just a few more years. Yet when the cancer recurred several years later, Carol believed she already had been granted those extra years she had wanted so much. She didn't want the chemotherapy to rob her family of positive memories of her in her final days. She refused all treatment and soon died.

Did one choice or the other cause Carol to miss God's ultimate plan for her life? I don't think so.

You Can't Hurry the Process

Process is defined as "a natural phenomenon marked by gradual changes that lead toward a particular result; a series of actions or operations conducing to an end." *Conducing* means "to bring about a particular and usually desirable result."

Let's think about the word *desirable*. As hard as it might seem to believe, the Bible and science both point to the fact that chaos is good for us. That's what the process is all about.

You may be choking at that thought. "Chaos, *good?* Right!" Maybe you're thinking about your mother forcing you to eat your spinach because it was "good for you." Or the doctor insisting on medicine because "it will make you feel better."

But it's true. Even medical science supports the notion: "Over the last few years, researchers have learned that . . . by making small adjustments to one of the parameters governing a system's behavior, they can subdue the erratic motions of the irregular rhythms of a beating heart or seemingly random patterns in the electrical activity of nerve cells." In other words, introducing even the smallest element of chaos to an already present state of chaos can bring healing. Some medical records report that irregular heartbeats have been corrected not by slowing down the patient's heart to the point of calmness, but by injecting chaos. "Sometimes, a system may require chaotic behavior rather than strictly periodic behavior in order to function properly. For example, some medical researchers have suggested that extreme regularity can lead to certain types of heart failure and brain seizures."[5]

Amazing, isn't it? The very chaos we try so hard to eliminate seems to be an imperative good in our lives. Part of God's process for our benefit.

What Is "Good"?

I went to the hairdresser yesterday and decided to change my hairstyle after fifteen years. (Maybe this topic had an impact.) As I settled into the chair, I overheard a man and woman discussing the weather. (Why do we always discuss the weather when we don't know what else to say? Certainly there must be more interesting things we share.) The dark-haired beauty observed, "It sure is a gorgeous fall day."

"It sure is," remarked the blue-eyed gentleman.

"We've had a remarkably mild summer," continued the beauty.
"Yeah, and the spring was wonderful, too."
"Oh, no." They seemed to speak in unison, dread in their voices, "I guess we'd better prepare for a hard winter."
"Yeah, you watch. We'll have to pay our dues. Things can't go well for *two* years straight," the woman concluded.

As I listened to their animated dialogue, I wondered why we always assume change and chaos are bad? Why is resistance to future events always our first response? Why can't we embrace them? Like rock climbers who lose their footing, we're frightened, vulnerable, and helpless to confront the future with peace and confidence. It's as though we're the victims of fate's whim rather than the recipients of the Creator's care.

As we've seen, the apostle Paul made a remarkable statement describing God's work in the process of life: "God causes all things to work together for good to those who love God, to those who are called according to His purpose."[6] Paul didn't offer this as a false hope. This is gritty, hard-edged truth. If we've placed our faith in Jesus Christ, we've acknowledged our love for God and responded to his claim on our life.

So what does "all things work together for good" mean? That's the puzzle. Recently, as I viewed the situation of a friend, I was thinking, *God, this is* not *good. I don't understand what's happening. How can this be a good thing?*

It seemed the voice of God spoke to my heart, "And Linda, what *is* good? Can you define it? Who are you to determine what is and is not good when I am the source of goodness? It originated with me. It is my character quality. And I'm the only one who knows its definition. I'm the only one who knows what is really good, isn't that right?"

That stopped me in my tracks. I had a lot to think about.

"No one is good but God," Jesus said. So I guess he's the only one who knows what is good. And though a thing may not look good, that doesn't mean it can't *be* good. So it goes with chaos. The chaotic thing we confront may be something we can't imagine as being good. Yet from God's perspective, it may be necessary for our growth and joy in life—whether it resulted from an act of evil, a circumstance of life in a broken world, or an act of God. He has the power to take it and transform it into a good thing.

That's what he promises to do. All things—not some, not a few, not when God feels like it—but all things combine, blend, and change for our good. It's God's process.

Process and the Will of God

As I speak at meetings throughout the nation, Christians often come forward and ask about God's will, either concerning big issues or the simple details of daily existence. What is God's will? Is there a perfect will of God? If so, can we permanently miss it? And if we miss it, will we reap the consequences for a lifetime? Will we be placed on a shelf until death? And if the perfect will of God can be missed, is there a permissive will of God?

There are other questions. If God's plan is something we call Plan A, then what happens when we make our own Plan B? These questions and my gynecologist's concerns compelled me to do an extensive search in the Bible for the facts concerning the will of God. What is his will in this Step 4 we call the process of life? How does chaos affect the will of God? Do our responses to chaos change anything? How does this all relate to the process?

If the perfect will of God is a straight path we must walk—from which we must never stray—we'll never find it. But as we've already seen, life with God is not a walk on a tightrope, dominated by rules and requirements. That's legalism. Instead, the Christian life is a vibrant, living, ongoing encounter with God. A process.

Each of us is in the process (justification, sanctification, and glorification are the theological words so often used), and God's will unfolds and embraces us during the process. God's will is his purpose for us, flowing from his heart—more a concept of his person to be grasped and experienced than a narrowly constructed walkway to which we rigidly adhere.

To be sure, the way *into* a relationship with God is narrow. The Bible makes it clear that we enter only through Jesus. But after that step is taken, the Christian life is depicted as a process of endless possibilities orchestrated and inhabited by God.

Designing the Process

How does God accomplish his will in the midst of the life process? By conforming all things to his purposes. God's will is not a static thing but a living activity. Paul explains in Ephesians 1:11, "In him we were also chosen, having been predestined according to the plan of him *who works out everything in conformity with the purpose of his will.*"

Jesus speaks with great tenderness on this subject. "Are not two sparrows sold for a penny? Yet not one of them will fall to the ground apart from the will of your Father. And even the very hairs of your head are all numbered. So don't be afraid, you are worth more than many sparrows."[7]

As we make choices within the scheme of God's will for us, we can make good choices (those according to God's biblical instructions) and bad choices (that go against his words). Obedience is always Plan A.

Let's look again at the biblical story of Sarah. She wanted a child. Even though her husband Abraham insisted that God promised them an heir, they remained childless. Waiting for God to fulfill that promise would have been Plan A.

But instead, Sarah took matters into her own hands, urging Abraham to father a child by her servant girl, Hagar. The girl bore Ishmael, whom Sarah accepted as her own.

But Plan B choices always have consequences. Ishmael brought Sarah, Hagar, and Abraham much pain. Ishmael's descendants became enemies of the nation that descended from Isaac, the promised son Sarah eventually bore. The current Mideast struggle is a continuation of that rivalry.

But did Sarah's Plan B action thwart, hinder, or stop the will of God for all time and eternity? Or for her? Absolutely not. Her son was born in spite of her age, doubts, and poor choices.

Sure, there are times when God's will is clearly seen. A church or a family or an individual Christian makes a major decision because God leads in some big, obvious way. But more often, God's will is discovered through daily "continuing on" in relationship with him.[8]

Many years ago, when I lived in Hamilton, Massachusetts, I got to know the great theologian Harold Ockenga. One day as I took him to the airport, he made a very simple statement about God's will. "You can only know it when you give your life to God, live a lifetime, and then look back." I stared at him without a clue as to his meaning.

He chuckled at my surprise. "Read Romans 12:1–2." I did. It reads, "Therefore, I urge you, brothers, in view of God's mercy, to offer your bodies as living sacrifices, holy and pleasing to God—this is your spiritual act of worship. Do not conform any longer to the pattern of this world, but be transformed by the renewing of your mind. Then you will be able to test and approve what God's will is—his good, pleasing and perfect will."

So you see, it seems that we will grasp the will of God as we participate with him in the process of our lives. And most of what we see will be in retrospect. "*Then* you will be able," the text reads. When we look back and survey the landscape of a lifetime, we will see the intricate weaving of God's will and plan made real in and through us. Meanwhile, experiencing his will comes when we live day by day as his friends, giving ourselves to him while walking with him.

So in summary, the will of God is the process. It is a journey to be experienced more than a path to be located. There may be detours through Plan B choices that are counter to God's clear commands, but even these are woven into the journey when we turn from them and return to the Bible for direction. Only if we refuse to believe or refuse to turn back will we miss the great

Discovering the Will of God in the Process of Life

Certain truths that define the will of God are listed here to help us reach a clearer understanding of the process of life.

1. Jesus alone is perfect. As long as we live on this earth, we'll never be perfect. Our nature is to sin and rebel against God's direction in our life. Yet when we believe in him, Jesus continues to transform us. Still, perfection is found only in heaven, where we will live with Christ forever.
2. God's standard is perfection. "Be perfect, therefore, as your heavenly Father is perfect" (Matt. 5:48).
3. Perfection is unattainable in this life. Even the old covenant law failed to make this possible, but in Christ, perfection is a continuous experience to be pursued by the Holy Spirit's process until its fulfillment in heaven. (See Phil. 3:12; Heb. 10:1; 7:11; 8:7–13.)
4. Salvation is the first step toward experiencing the will of God. Before time began, God initiated his huge redemptive plan to restore sinful humanity. It will come to completion when Jesus returns. God's re-

demptive plan for history is the "whole will of God" (Acts 20:27). As it relates to our lives, we begin to understand and enter the will of God when we place our faith in Christ for salvation. (See Eph. 1:5, 9; Acts 22:14–16; Heb. 10:10; John 6:40.)

5. The "will of God" as it relates to our daily lives is more the act of being and doing in response to God than a path to be followed. God's will is a reflection of his character. Walking with God through the Holy Spirit's power is walking within God's will. (See Eph. 5:17; 6:6; 2 Cor. 8:5; Col. 1:9; 4:12; 1 Thess. 4:3; and 1 Peter 2:15.)

God's will is not as much a path as a purpose, a state of being, expansive in scope. It is unlimited because God has no limits.

And so, as far as your choices are concerned, there's really no distinction between God's perfect will and his permissive will—just between Plan A and Plan B. Plan A occurs when we make choices consistent with God's direction in the Bible. Plan B happens when we disobey. But all choices fall within God's will. His perfect will is an ongoing thing, constantly being experienced and worked out as we travel through life with him. Everything is within this perfect will under his control and his sovereignty. His perfect will is not a tightrope to be balanced upon but a relationship to be maintained.

process and purposes of our destiny. All is contained within God's greater will—his sovereign plan.

I find a great deal of peace in these words. I can stop working so hard, fixing the present, regretting the past, and fearing the future. Instead, I can trust that God will fit everything together for good in the end.

Choose Your Own Adventure

Life in process reminds me a little of the *Choose Your Own Adventure* novels my children loved to read as elementary students. A plot would begin and, at certain points in the story, the child could choose the next turn of events in the plot. Yet with each choice, the plot twisted like a road that, while winding, would reach the same destination. Life is similar. I've drawn a simple diagram to illustrate the process. This illustration demonstrates three possible paths for one life, demonstrating how immediate choices and ongoing choices caused detours and how Plan A or Plan B choices at crucial junctures affected the path (see diagram).

So why is thinking in boxes so harmful? Why are all our structures and blindness strategies so devastating? Because in our attempt to provide immediate solutions to every problem, we start to think we can't go on with life until the issue at hand, whatever it might be, is resolved. We obsess about it, lose sleep over it, stop enjoying life until this albatross is removed.

What if it never goes away? What if it's simply a part of the life we have been given, intended to be integrated into the fabric of our existence? What then?

When we refuse to accept the process and resist chaos by creating human alternatives to somehow tame this pulsating force of creation, we actually hinder our progress. All our efforts only survive for a moment, anyway. They may become deceptions poised to attack like a rattler coiled to strike. Why? Because they refuse the possibility of beneficial change and transformation.

Have you ever noticed God's tenderness in sending Adam and Eve out of the garden? In their sinful state, if they had eaten from

Finding Peace in the Process

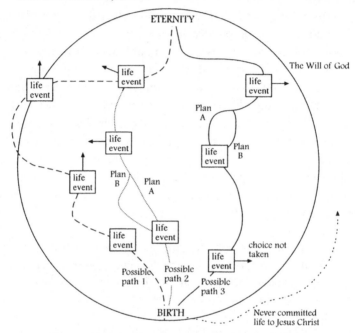

THE WILL OF GOD

PLAN OF GOD His work is to conform everything with his purposes—"who works out everything in conformity with the purpose of his will" (Eph. 1:11).

PROMISE OF GOD His accomplishment of his will, will not be stopped—"No plan of Yours will be thwarted" (Job 42:2).

the Tree of Life Eternal, their broken condition—and ours— would have become permanent. Instead, God sealed the promise of transformation by keeping them away from the Tree of Life Eternal.[9] With their banishment from the garden, the possibility of change and redemption became a permanent reality.

When we choose to recognize chaos, accepting rather than resisting it, we consent to participate in the dance, the process of transformation. Only by embracing the process do we find peace.

Transformation in the Process

Have you ever experienced something that seemed to be the very event you feared most? Devastated by its chaotic intervention, you flinched in pain. You wrestled uselessly to free yourself from its hold. Finally, you simply began the process of surrender. You gave the situation to God. You abandoned your idolatrous systems and clung to God in the process.

In time the event faded, woven intricately into life's fabric. It intermingled so completely that it's impossible to imagine life without it. Finally, one day you were able to look back and see positive results rising out of what seemed to be anything but a positive situation. Beauty and design were birthed from chaos.

The truth of the Chaos Factor, this intervention in everyday life, is that if you accept it, your life is enriched and enlarged. I know it's true because many people have shared their stories with me. As an instructor, I travel the globe teaching these principles, and I count it a great privilege to meet these people and hear their stories. Some allow me to share glimpses of their lives with others. Here is Robin's story.

On September 14, 1993, the birth of our son, our fifth child, changed our lives. He was born with Down syndrome and suffered a stroke at some point around birth. He was in the children's hospital for two weeks in the NICU [neonatal intensive care unit].

What happened next really happened to us. Through this experience, we discovered a greater awareness of a God who loves us and is in control, our eyes were opened to the frailty of life, and we acquired a greater thankfulness for modern medicine and technology.

Our son is doing well now and, at age two, is starting to be a slight "tornado" of his own. He just started walking and is really a fun guy to be around.

How do we cope? We take one step at a time and are so amazed, thrilled, yes, actually thankful for everything he accomplishes.

You asked about one event that changed our life. This isn't a one-time event. Our change is ever-changing. We are still learning. Since our son's disability, we have a greater acceptance for people of every kind. I still struggle with seeing life on a different path than the one I planned. But God is using this to change me. I've learned to trust him. Rest in God. Take one day at a time. And rely on the truth psalm-writer David wrote centuries ago, "For you created my inmost being; you knit me together in my mother's womb. I praise you because I am fearfully and wonderfully made; your works are wonderful, I know that full well."

God uses the chaos of life to create something beautiful in the process. As a result, we learn new things, grow in our understanding, and are changed in a way that ultimately benefits us. The Chaos Factor is a friend to be embraced throughout life, rather than an enemy to deny or avoid.

And when we look back, we can look with gratitude. Henri Nouwen writes in his book *Here and Now,*

> How can we live a truly grateful life? When we look back at all that has happened to us, we easily divide our lives into good things to be grateful for and bad things to forget. But with a past thus divided, we cannot move freely into the future. With many things to forget we can only limp toward the future.
>
> True spiritual gratitude embraces all of our past, the good as well as the bad events, the joyful as well as the sorrowful moments. From the place where we stand, everything that took place brought us to this place, and we want to remember all of it as part of God's guidance. That does not mean that all that happened in the past was good, but it does mean that even the bad didn't happen outside the loving presence of God.[10]

The remainder of our journey will offer practical ways to prepare for and respond positively to the chaos that confronts us. We will take the next step by learning how to let go. Whether watching a kindergartner leave for the first day of school, or standing by silently while a spouse or child insists on making an unnecessary mistake, learning to give up control is one of life's most difficult challenges. Let's discover new and exciting ways to relinquish control and continue our travel through chaos.

7

Learning to Let Go

The Act of Giving Up Control

Much of our ability to experience inner peace and happiness rests with our willingness to accept change. Change is the very essence of life. When we accept change—and encourage it—we are in the flow of life.

Susan L. Taylor

Spring *burst into* full bloom, seemingly overnight. Daffodils nodded their golden heads while red tulips stood erect, radiant in their beauty. Dogwoods bowed their snowy blossoms to the wind's caress. The regal elegance of scarlet azaleas outlined every roadway. The freshness of new life flooded my soul.

Two years and six months after Carol's death, I realized I could feel again. I had chosen to accept rather than resist the chaos that ransacked my life. I was continuing the process of turning away from my coping mechanisms, turning toward trust. Sorrow blended into the fabric of life and its knifing pain faded.

But there were more lessons to learn, more insights to embrace. I felt like a teenager before the prom, stumbling to learn new dance steps—steps for this chaos waltz. I had mastered a few steps, but I'd merely attempted others. Still, it was time to combine the individual movements and glide across the floor. It was time to waltz.

"Take care of Bill and the boys," Carol begged two weeks before her death. After asking everyone else to leave the room, she returned to the subject. "Care for them. Promise me you will take my place and be there for them." I'd never understood the power of a deathbed request until that day. I loved her—her life had enriched mine and I owed her my promise in response. So I agreed. I accepted her commission, and it reshaped my life.

For the next two-and-a-half years, I became mother to her sons. They became a part of my family. I suddenly had five children instead of three, and I loved them all. When teacher's conferences were required, I conferred. When softball, football, and tennis games were played, I sat in the bleachers. When tutoring became necessary, I taught. Birthdays, holidays, shopping trips—I incorporated them into my life. I loved them like my own, and all for Carol. Where was Carol's husband? Working, grieving, caring for his boys, trying to cope.

Then Bill met someone and everything changed. Like the bride of a mother's firstborn son, this woman couldn't have been good enough. Though I never met her, I didn't like her. Of course it had nothing to do with her. It was all about me and Carol. After all these months of caring, mothering, loving on Carol's behalf, I felt betrayed. And somehow I felt Carol was betrayed, too.

I had a new dilemma with Bill and the boys. Should I befriend the woman who would elbow me out of their family, or should I stubbornly withhold any support of Bill's new relationship?

After all I had done for them, I didn't want to lose them—but I knew I'd lose them either way.

As I brooded over this, I had an epiphany, a moment of sudden insight. I flashed back to a seminar I had attended several years earlier. A sophisticated, brown-haired woman in her fifties, face wrinkled by sun and smiles, stood up and began her lecture, "I am probably one of the most controlling women you will ever meet. We're all controlling, you know. It's part of the human framework. One of the best things that can happen for us is to realize our desire to control and learn to let go."

I remember being rather shocked and appalled. *What woman in her right mind would ever call herself controlling, much less announce it to the world? I can't imagine a more terrible thing said about anyone. It's certainly not true of me.*

But now I knew she was right: we're all controlling. It's our defense against chaos. Even when we've identified faulty coping mechanisms and abandoned them, we still want control over our lives and the lives of others. We assume we know what's best, and we do all we can to create that "best" situation for ourselves and those around us. I did not want Bill involved with that woman. After all, I was a better mother. I knew what Carol wanted for her kids. If anyone would fill in for Carol, I was the best one for the job.

When I think back on it, I wonder why anyone put up with me. Were my intentions good? The best. Was I acting out of love? I certainly thought so. All I wanted was for Carol's sons to be happy and healthy, growing up strong and confident. And I exerted untold hours of loving and caring to help them do this. But I guess all my giving carried a price. I wanted control. I didn't want to see them fail, make mistakes, or get hurt. I wanted them to have a perfect, happily-ever-after life and was certain I was the one to give it to them.

Sometimes chaos enters your life when other people make decisions you have no control over, decisions that are rightfully theirs to make. Bill insisted on bringing this woman into his family, and no insight, wisdom, or advice on my part was going to change his mind. Of course he was right. I was hurt, but I had to let go.

105

"It seems unfair that pain is the price we pay for caring," writes Carol Kuykendall in *Learning to Let Go*.[1] And it did seem unfair, but I realized I had no right to impose my choices on Bill or his sons, no matter how much I cared for them. I had to give up control, letting them experience their destiny as it would unfold for them.

"Letting go contradicts our instincts," Kuykendall adds. "It is painful. Letting go is bewildering. We feel ambivalent. Sometimes we long for the anticipated peace (of letting a person go to make their own decisions and walk their own destiny) while other times we can't imagine life without the person."[2]

Letting go of Carol was one of the most painful things I've ever had to do. First I was forced to let cancer take her, and then I had to let go of her family, losing my ability to fulfill the deathbed promise that had kept my life intertwined with hers. Both of these occasions brought chaos; suddenly things were out of my control.

Letting go demands that we rise above our own feelings, no matter how powerful they are. We may feel we know the best course of action, and we may feel that the world will disintegrate if this course is not followed, but it's not always up to us. Sometimes other people get to decide.

As I realized this, and as I slowly yielded control, I gained a great new freedom. I didn't have to monitor everyone else's choices anymore. Their decisions were their business. I could be objective.

Yes, giving up control and learning to let go can be excruciatingly difficult, but the freedom and release on the other side of relinquishment is inexpressible. I began to exercise this newfound freedom in other relationships, especially with my husband and children, and it was transforming.

I remembered that their future is in God's hands, not mine. They are responsible for their own choices. Sure, I could continue to mentor, offer insights and suggestions, but their choices were ultimately between them and God. I learned to rest in that. Parenting was no longer a pass-or-fail test I was terrified of failing for fear it would destroy their lives. Parenting became a pleasure. I was no longer the controlling, demanding mom I'm sure I seemed before. I could simply love them. It wasn't so important that I impose my will on them. I could trust God's will in their lives instead.

Since my revelation that beautiful day in May, I've tried to teach others the lesson I learned so painfully. I know I'm not alone in this. Giving up control is the most popular topic in my seminars. Why? We all want to cling to control over life. We have our agendas and we want them carried out. Some will risk anything to be sure their idea of what is best is followed. When we are forced to let go, by circumstances or by other people's choices, we're hurt. We wonder how God could let this happen. But as we learn to give up control on a regular basis, we find freedom and joy.

"I can't tell you how many nights I've lain awake worrying about my children," exclaimed one woman at the end of a weekend conference I led. "They've all left for college and I don't have any idea what they're doing. I don't know where they're going, who they're with, or if they're all right. It's driving me crazy."

The rest of us in the room knew what she was saying. Our sense of control over our kids is very strong. But this woman went on to talk about what she'd learned at this conference: "Now I realize that being a good mom doesn't have to mean you worry yourself sick. I understand the difference between my responsibility versus control over their lives. I slept last night eight hours without waking. It was the best night's sleep I've had in months."

For generations, control disguised as responsibility has dominated and destroyed lives and relationships. Chaos precipitates it, and our iron wills maintain it. As this mother learned, there is freedom in discovering we are responsible only for our own decisions and actions. We can encourage others, love them, and advise them, but the responsibility ultimately is theirs. They must make their own choices about their future. We can trust the Divine Orchestrator of life to keep them secure in his care.

Giving up control continues to be one of the greatest challenges of my life. It will be for you, too. But the rest of this book will offer steps to help you join the dance.

The Nuances of Chaos

Chaos ensures that life cannot be controlled. Only when we accept this fact can we understand the futility of our attempts. Then we can give up.

Imagine the chaos of, say, a movie star's schedule. One magazine article I read on an airplane recently offered a glimpse behind the scenes, giving us a picture of chaos and attempted control. First it focused on Tom Leonardis, Whoopi Goldberg's personal assistant: "You see people like Leonardis all over Hollywood, driving the boss's Ford Explorer to the dry cleaners, the bank, the gourmet pet-food store. Their tools include detailed 'limo logs' and to-the-nanosecond appointment calendars, as well as portable phones, faxes, computers, and Rolodexes. On any given day, they'll screen hundreds of calls, make last-minute restaurant or plane reservations, then reshuffle all the other hair/make-up/shrink appointments so their celeb can go through what appears to be a seamless, streamlined, movie-star kind of day."

How does Leonardis control the chaos? "Manila file folders."

Nick Nolte, on the other hand, is "messy, messy," the author reports. "His office—it's like a tornado hit it, though he knows exactly where every piece of paper is." Nolte's assistant confesses that if she lost her Franklin Day Planner, "I might fall off the face of the earth."[3] Each assistant attempts to conquer chaos, but without complete success. The greatest amount of energy is exerted adjusting to the fact that chaos won't be conquered. Constant changes are demanded.

Let's find out why.

Chaos, Chaos Everywhere

We've already looked at the research underlying chaos theory. A butterfly flapping its wings in Borneo causes rain in Brooklyn—that sort of thing. Researchers determined that weather is ultimately unpredictable, resulting in the same for all of life.

There are just too many factors to take into account. You can't measure all the butterflies!

But what if you could?

In *Turbulent Mirror,* Briggs and Peat explain this development. "Chaos was merely complexity so great that in practice scientists couldn't track it, but they were sure that in principle they might one day be able to do so. When that day came, there would be no chaos, so to speak, only Newton's laws. It was a spellbinding idea."[4]

So build a smart enough computer and maybe you *can* count all those butterflies. If you can add up all the physical factors that affect the weather (and everything else in the world), you should still be able to predict everything. So went this "spellbinding" idea, slavishly bound to Newtonian, linear, cause-effect thinking.

"Turbulence, irregularity, and unpredictability are everywhere," the authors continue, "but it has always seemed fair to assume that this was 'noise,' a messiness that resulted from the way things in reality crowd into each other. Put another way, chaos has been thought to be the result of a complexity that in theory could be stripped down to its orderly underpinnings. Now scientists are discovering that this assumption was mistaken."[5]

Chaos will not be removed. With the emergence of computers able to track scientific study to a degree beyond anything imagined, the world has proved to be not *more* predictable but *less* so. Briggs and Peat say that scientists are downplaying their "traditional concern with prediction, control, and the analysis of parts" in favor of "a new concern for the way the unpredictable whole of things moves."[6] Science isn't interested in removing chaos anymore but learning more about it.

Science is discovering about the physical world the same thing we've been learning about our personal world: beneath what we've always assumed to be our well-ordered world is a pulsating underworld of chaos. Life becomes an exciting, stimulating experience of unrealized opportunity and new possibilities as we incorporate the reality of chaos into our daily existence. Chaos is life itself.

Jules-Henri Poincare, brilliant French mathematician, physicist, and philosopher, was onto this in the nineteenth century.

Studying the movement of planets, which everyone assumed were fixed in their rotation and axis, "Poincare discovered that with even the very smallest perturbation [disturbance], some orbits behaved in an erratic, even chaotic way. His calculations showed that a minute gravitational pull from a third body might cause a planet to wobble and weave drunkenly in its orbit and even fly out of the solar system altogether. It now appeared that a system sealed in a box and left untouched for billions of years could at any moment develop its own instabilities and chaos . . . even a completely determined system like the orbiting planets could have indeterminate results."[7] Chaos may affect our lives at any moment. It will not be confined or controlled.

The Divine Conductor of Chaos

Research again proves the activity of divine orchestration. Some power greater than we can comprehend holds planets in place, molecules in cohesion, and all of existence intact.

It's fascinating that this chaos, controlled by the Superforce of creation, is so rarely acknowledged, though it remains so pervasive. "It's daunting to think," write Briggs and Peat, "how many places turbulence occurs in nature: in air currents, in fast-flowing rivers swirling around rocks and the supports for bridges, in the way hot lava flows from a volcano, in weather disasters such as typhoons and tidal waves."[8]

Chaos in nature has been an object of fascination for great minds throughout the ages, yet we rarely prepare for it or anticipate its possible consequences.

"Turbulence often causes problems for humans. It interferes in our technology by jostling the movement of oil in pipelines; it jars the behavior of pumps and turbines, of trucks on highways, of ships' hulls in the water, and the coffee in passengers' jet cups."[9]

Some scientists continue searching for a name for this superforce, described so easily by Paul the apostle. Jesus Christ, Paul writes, "is the image of the invisible God, the firstborn over all creation. For by him all things were created: things in heaven and on earth, visible and invisible. . . . He is before all things, and in him all things hold together."[10]

Jesus alone controls the chaos.

From Chaos Arises Order

Chaos resists our control, and yet remarkable new studies prove that from the chaos arises a subtle order. This effect was first seen by John Russell, a Scottish engineer and ship designer in 1834. He witnessed a strange event while observing the movement of a wave in the wake of a small boat passing in a narrow channel of water. As he waited for the wave to break down, it instead gained momentum. With each foot it traveled, it reacted with the water, seeming to gain energy from the chaos stirred in the channel to continue its flow. The wave integrated the chaos into form.

We see this amazing occurrence daily. For example, let's say you leave work a bit early. Though you notice a moderate flow of traffic, your driving isn't affected by it very much. But, as Briggs and Peat note, "toward 4 o'clock, traffic becomes heavier and we begin to react and interact with the other drivers. At a certain critical point we begin to be 'driven' by the total traffic pattern. The traffic has become a self-organizing system."[11] We become part of the pattern.

Chaos will not be controlled. And our iron-fisted insistence on asserting control not only frustrates us but becomes a hindrance to the subtle order God is orchestrating from the chaos. Rather than acting on some exaggerated sense of responsibility to control the chaos, we should recognize it is our privilege to integrate chaos into the flow of our lives. Like it or not, we must walk the path of change. The key is allowing flexibility and sensitivity to determine the boundary between our responsibility and the responsibilities of others.

Peter Senge, a social scientist at MIT's Sloan School who works with Systems Dynamics Group, writes, "Learning to handle complexity [of chaos] means learning to live more intuitively, because intuition is the key to making significant changes in complex systems, helping them evolve, and evolving with them."[12]

The six stages of change will help us understand this process.

The Six Stages of Change

With his colleagues, psychologist James O. Prochaska, director of the Cancer Prevention Research Center at the University of Rhode Island, conducted more than fifty studies of human response to change in thousands of individuals. The team defined six stages of change: precontemplation, contemplation, preparation, action, maintenance, and termination.

1. Precontemplation. The precontemplation stage is denial. "This is not happening to me!" It's the way most of us initially react to major changes, especially traumatic or negative ones. We cannot contemplate it yet. We need time to get our minds ready for the onslaught. It's the blindness method of chaos resistance.

The problem occurs when people stay in this stage too long. We've already discussed denial in the form of blindness. But this precontemplation also takes the form of blaming, another evasive maneuver. Sometimes, when we're forced to face a change, we still deny our responsibility to deal with it. Rather than addressing the situation, we blame life, the world, those around us, and God for the chaotic interruption, and we wait for any of the above to fix things.

I hope this book has helped you get past this first step. You should be at least contemplating the chaos that is regularly changing your life.

2. Contemplation. "Contemplators recognize the problem, try to understand it and begin to make plans to alter behavior, although those plans are indefinite," writes Deborah Shelton in her article, "The Power to Change," commenting on the Rhode Island research.[13] In this stage, we understand that resisting chaos is not

Learning to Let Go

only futile, but harmful. As we've already seen, our resistance methods can be detrimental to our health and sanity, and they can often become forms of idolatry. In contemplation, we finally face the chaos, putting aside all our efforts to avoid it. We recognize that we have to do something about it, and we prepare to do so.

3. Preparation. Here's where we get down to business. Our vague preparations become specific. "The preparation stage involves setting a date for action and publicly announcing the intended behavioral change," Prochaska says about the Rhode Island findings.[14]

This book, I trust, has helped you to contemplate the many changes in your life rather than resist them. I hope you've identified with those whose stories have been told, seeing how they learned to adjust to chaos—giving up their protective mechanisms and accepting the changes God brings them. By now, you may be ready to make some adjustments of your own.

As the book continues, I'll be asking you to make specific choices about your behavioral change. I hope you'll write these choices down. Discuss them with a trusted friend or colleague, someone you feel will keep your confidence and yet will encourage you in your new attitudes and actions.

4. Action. The next stage is the active, exciting stage. Wonderful things can happen. Yet this stage takes time. It's part of the process. It requires a strong step into a new way of thinking and being. Researchers claim that the action level requires the greatest amount of time, energy, and commitment.

Here we begin the final steps of our journey into chaos. We'll discuss the fifth and sixth stages—maintenance and termination—in chapter 11, but now we'll pause in the change process to consider the final action steps of the Chaos Factor. The next step, Step 5, is to let go of your control.

Letting Go

That sounds so simple, doesn't it? But you know as well as I do that it's one of our most difficult choices.

Remember this scenario from a few chapters back? Your unmarried teenage daughter announces that she's pregnant. Your response is to organize the chaos by sending her to Aunt Mary's until the birth and then put the child up for adoption. Everything nicely ordered. The secret is kept. But at no time in this example have you sought outside counsel or requested the insight and power of God. You try to conquer the chaos by controlling the situation and everyone in it.

Step 5: Let go of your control.

I know a family that faced this very situation and took these actions. Yet just recently I met another family whose members took a different approach. They listened to the daughter's concerns. She realized the boy was unfit to be a father, and they shared her disappointment. She feared the changes this would cause in her life and goals, and they shared those fears. She didn't know what to do, and they shared her confusion. The family gathered around her to offer support. They gave her freedom to choose her path.

Her parents helped her consider her options. They assured her that they trusted her ability to make the necessary decisions. When I first spoke with this young mother-to-be, she outlined the options she saw and said she had decided to put the child up for adoption. Her family support was evident in her decision.

When I saw Jennifer (not her real name) again two months before the birth, she confided that she was going to keep her baby. She would still be able to work because her mother offered to watch the child during her work hours. Although still frightened by the unknown future, she was at peace. Family support provided her the strength and freedom she needed to handle the chaos and integrate it into the flow of life.

Learning to Let Go

The thing I found most assuring was her description of family support. Jennifer knew that this had brought sadness and concern to her parents. She was not treating it lightly. She had feared telling her father about the pregnancy at first, but he responded with love and support rather than condemnation and anger. Then her parents gave the greatest gift of all: they allowed her to make her own choices. Rather than imposing their choices and trying to control her behavior, they gave her the freedom to choose. And that's one of the first steps to giving up control in the midst of chaos—recognizing that we are responsible only for our own choices.

Does this mean we can't offer advice? Isn't it our responsibility as parents to direct our children's behavior because our experiences make us older and wiser? I often hear these rebuttals when I teach these concepts, and they usually come from parents with an exaggerated sense of responsibility. I know. I was one.

I discovered a chart that helps delineate healthy responsibility from responsibility that stifles and hinders. Where do you find yourself in this outline?

When I feel responsible FOR others...	When I feel responsible TO others...
I fix by...	*I show empathy by...*
protecting	encouraging
rescuing	sharing
controlling	being open to discussion
carrying their feelings	being sensitive
tuning them out	listening
I feel...	*I feel...*
tired	relaxed
anxious	free
fearful	aware
liable	have high self-esteem
I am concerned with...	*I am concerned with...*
the solution	relating person to person
answers	feelings
circumstances	the individual as a person with unique gifts, abilities, needs, and desires
being right	
details	
performance	

Continued

Continued

When I feel responsible FOR others ...
I am a controller. I expect the person to live up to my expectations.

When I feel responsible TO others ...
I believe if I share myself, the other person has enough inner resources to make it. I am a helper-guide. I expect the person to be responsible for himself or herself and his or her actions. I can trust and let go.

This chart distinguishes between caring and controlling. Caring gives freedom to the people who are cared for—freedom to make their own decisions. The consequences of their actions are their own responsibility. Regardless of these consequences, the caring person remains a true and supportive friend.

Does this mean that the caring person condones or agrees with the individual's choices or behavior? Not necessarily. But it does mean the caring person's genuine concern for the individual remains constant regardless.

I recently saw this demonstrated when a friend asked me for advice. Her brother was getting married and she was responsible for the housing arrangements during the event. Her unmarried sister was living with a boyfriend at the time. This sister wanted to attend the wedding and sleep with her boyfriend in the same room of my friend's home.

My friend felt trapped. She and her husband didn't agree with the sister's lifestyle, and they had four small children who would ask difficult questions about these arrangements. While they didn't want to alienate the sister, they also didn't want their children to think they condoned this behavior.

They decided to welcome the sister to their home but not to let her share a room with her boyfriend. They explained to her that what she did anywhere else was her business, but they wanted to preserve certain standards in their home. To my friend's surprise, the sister was not offended. Though the sister didn't share my friend's values, she respected them. She and her boyfriend chose to stay in the home in separate bedrooms. My friend continued to love and care for her sister unconditionally without condoning her sister's choices—but not trying to control her life either. Caring rather than controlling enables all parties to take responsibility for their choices and the consequences while maintaining an unhindered concern for others.

Unhealthy control assumes many subtle forms. We can control with our silence, body language, or simple expressions. Statistics show that 80 percent of communication is nonverbal. It's important to recognize these methods of control. If, every time you argue, you give your spouse the silent treatment until he or she accepts your will, this is your method of control. Remaining distant and unapproachable may communicate your disapproval as strongly as shouting or stomping out of the house.

Perhaps you manipulate people and events to bring about a predetermined end. Consider the couple who want a single friend to meet Mr. or Miss Right. They continue creating situations that force encounters with eligible strangers. Well-meaning efforts, maybe. Controlling, definitely.

Letting go of unhealthy control and giving up this exaggerated sense of responsibility are among the healthiest actions you will take. New possibilities explode on your horizon as your view of chaos shifts. Chaos becomes an interesting acquaintance bringing fascinating opportunities whenever it arrives.

Susan L. Taylor, editor-in-chief of *Essence* magazine, writes, "Once we accept that it's time to move on with our lives and keep growing, we discover a new way of being and are made stronger by the experience. A great change occurring in our lives can mean giving birth to a richer, better self or to anxiety and depression. The degree of faith or resistance we bring to the experience determines which will be true for us. Trust God. Trust life. Nothing that is necessary for your growth and unfolding is ever taken away from you. Every experience in life is to help you discover your divine potential."[15]

Since I began to apply these concepts of choice, relinquishment of control, and trust, I have felt a new freedom. Freedom to live as I see best, hope the best for others, offer advice, but then set them free to live the way they are called to live. In rearing my children, I love them, encourage them, offer advice, and impart my trust to them—my trust in their ability to make good decisions. When asked about her parents, my nineteen-year-old, Ruthie, remarks that the most wonderful thing we gave her was our trust. She always knew we trusted her and believed she would make responsible decisions. She has never disappointed us.

Learning to let go is extremely important, because if we continue to impose our control over others' lives, our overprotective behavior stifles their ability to grow. Making choices strengthens us. We are forced to deal with the consequences of bad choices as well as good ones. Learning to consistently make good choices becomes essential, because our choices shape our lives. Carol Kuykendall writes,

> I learned that I have a responsibility not to allow my protective love to stifle the growth of my children. When we try to protect them from life's stings, we rob them of the opportunity to grow. Pain and suffering, more than joy, shape our lives and motivate us to learn and grow. We let go in obedience to God because we cannot control their lives; most importantly, we let go because we love them.
>
> It is the feeling of possession that causes us trouble when releasing. The more we possess something, whether an object or a person, the more pain we feel in letting go. We must hold on to everything, even our children, loosely.[16]

That's the key. Holding loosely. Letting go is one of the greatest expressions of love. Jennifer's parents let go. They loved Jennifer enough to let her make her own decisions in the midst of chaos. I let Bill and the boys go. It was the greatest expression of love I could offer. I knew I wanted what was best for them. Yes, Bill married and is happy. The boys and I keep in touch. We remain very close. Did it feel as though I was abandoning them? For a while, particularly when that exaggerated sense of responsibility kicked in, but in retrospect there is no question that it was best—the only thing to do. Chaos changed our lives, and so it should. We joined in the dance.

My friend Steve Brown told me of a conversation he had with a seminary student during his years as a professor. The young man said, "Dr. Brown, I have learned the four spiritual laws." Assuming he was speaking of a widely distributed pamphlet written years ago to explain the Christian faith, Steve was surprised that the young man hadn't learned these earlier. His puzzled expression tipped off the student.

"No, Dr. Brown," he said, "not those four spiritual laws. I've created new ones. They go like this: God alone is God. He is in charge. I am not. Repent."

Simple. To the point. True. God is God. We are not. It's about time we give up our need to take his place and control our world. It's time to turn to him—and repent.

As we've adopted this new perspective on chaos, a perspective that gives us the freedom to let go, we can continue in the process of integrating chaos. We can watch God bring new order out of chaos.

Integrating Daily Chaos into the Fabric of Life

> It is far better to recognize that we dwell in ambiguity. It is our homeland and should be accepted—even joyfully—all the while we paradoxically are trying to pierce its veil. This is what it is to be human—to live in an ambiguous world.
>
> Gerald F. Kreyche

The door slams as my last child leaves for school. Now I take a moment to regroup in preparation for the day's demands. What's on the schedule? Cleaning the kitchen, clothes washing, dinner preparations before taking off for a 10 A.M. seminar, 1 P.M. luncheon, 2 P.M. teacher's conference, 4 P.M. dental appointment, and grocery shopping. Why did I schedule so much on one day?

Oh well, better rev up that internal motor and shove the gears into fast forward. I can make it if I just keep moving.

It's 9:45 A.M. with three minutes to spare to cover the distance between my house and the seminar. I sling my pocketbook over my shoulder, grab the doorknob, rush across the threshold and ... *breeeeng* ... *breeeeng* ... *breeeeng* ... the phone.

Oh no! my brain screams. Not now. I just won't answer it. The machine will pick it up. But what if it's one of the kids? What if it's an emergency? Racing back through the doorway, I jerk the receiver off the hook. "Hello?"

"Hello, Linda, it's Marcia. Hi!"

Chaos Interrupts

What would you do, if you were in my tardy shoes? How do you handle the chaotic interruptions in your day? I must confess I've drastically changed. Several years ago, I would have quickly dismissed my caller, mumbling some excuse about being in a hurry and promising to call back later. I wouldn't wait to find out if Marcia needed something, had an emergency, or simply wanted to talk. I would rush back to the jammed schedule of my day, grumbling to myself all the way to the seminar about being late.

What about you?

Let's talk about the chaotic interruptions of daily life and create new strategies to deal with them, based on what we've been learning about chaos.

Those interruptions are necessary, believe it or not. Why? Because the alternative is utter boredom, and boredom is a killer. It's been proven: humans need change; predictability produces boredom. We all need mystery, some unexpected change. We hate it, but we love it. We hate it because we can't control it. We love it because it gives life.

Integrating Daily Chaos into the Fabric of Life

A friend recently described his experience in a sensory deprivation tank during a required experiment at graduate school. To understand human behavior, he was placed in a huge sealed cylinder devoid of stimuli. There was no light, no sound, no smell, nothing to touch, no movement. Nothingness. He explained that an extended period in this environment would produce insanity. Think about it. We all need to react to some stimuli.

Say you start reading a book but soon realize the plot is predictable. You put it down, right? Or you go to the movies and within five minutes you can guess the ending. You probably get up and leave. We need mystery and ambiguity.

Want to keep your marriage alive? Don't become so predictable that you are boring. You may find your spouse looking at someone else. Want to stay young in appearance and attitude? Don't become so set in your ways that you're a drag. You may find that your social invitations dwindle.

The chaotic interruptions that we curse are the very things that eliminate the predictable, remove boredom, insert ambiguity, create mystery, and give us life. And as we've learned from the Chaos Factor, these episodes precipitate a new design and order.

Medical science is finding this to be so important that scientists are searching for new ways to *interject* chaos into the human body to encourage development of this new design and order.

As described by one author, "William L. Ditto of the Georgia Institute of Technology in Atlanta and his coworkers have developed a scheme for *maintaining* chaos in a system. By slightly perturbing a system parameter according to a simple recipe, they can keep a system from ever settling into a repeating mode. The researchers describe this as an 'anti-control' technique."[1]

This research involves bodily systems, but did it ever cross your mind that the Divine Director is using the chaotic interventions in your everyday life to "slightly perturb" your schedule? Is he applying an anticontrol technique so a more beautiful design might arise? Chaos not only can produce anticontrol as a helpful tool for life, but it can actually relax or tame chaos in other situations where new patterns are sought.

Reporting on recent research, I. Peterson says, "Introducing random variability into certain types of systems can help tame their otherwise chaotic behavior." As a result, the scientist "got organized behavior patterns coming out of the system. The diversity, or disorder, provided a mechanism by which the system could organize itself."[2] In other words, the chaotic intrusions actually help to renew order in bodily systems when they go out of whack. Chaos not only eliminates control in some situations but, when interjected in other circumstances, creates order.

Mystery, ambiguity, and chaotic intervention now prove to be an essential for meaningful human life. Theologian Robert Cooley says, "Technologically, politically, demographically, economically, racially, morally and spiritually, unprecedented change is all about us and looms ahead. Each day brings fresh ambiguity."[3]

Ambiguous is defined as "doubtful or uncertain; capable of being understood in two or more ways." When your inconvenient telephone call occurs, you are doubtful of its meaning, unsure of its content or value. Who's calling? What do they want? You don't know. Any number of responses may be required of you.

You may need to drive to the school to pick up your sick child. Or you may quickly dismiss the caller, appearing rude, and that might create repercussions you'll have to deal with later. Or the call could be a major emergency that supersedes all your other plans. The result is an immediate and irrevocable adjustment in your day—not to mention your life, depending on the emergency.

Chaotic intervention removes the stale sameness that destroys life. It gives your life a new flavor. So in the same way we have viewed and applied the Chaos Factor as a universal, broad view of the scope of life, let's apply it as a clear, necessary response to the daily interruptions of life.

The Chaos Response to Daily Interruptions

Let's consider that phone call on my busy, busy day—or the last call that interrupted *you* when you were running out the door.

Integrating Daily Chaos into the Fabric of Life

Let's take each step of the Chaos Factor to discover new ways we can respond to it.

Step 1: Acknowledge that chaos is the raw material of life. Chaos happens. That telephone call should be no more a surprise than the fact that you eat and sleep. One way to respond differently is to begin to expect chaos and allow for it in your schedule. Since learning the Chaos Factor, I no longer leave myself only three minutes' leeway for arriving at any appointment. This required some major changes in my lifestyle.

First, I adjusted my timing. I now allow at least thirty minutes extra to arrive at my destination. Is this wasted time? Not at all. I simply relax in my preparations. I've found that leaving for an appointment early enables me to listen to an instructional tape as I drive. I may read a book, do research, or write if I have a few minutes to wait before the event begins.

If the telephone rings as I'm headed out the door, I'm prepared to embrace the chaos. I respond thoughtfully rather than anxiously. I am able to give my complete attention and interest to the person or situation.

Second, I began to reevaluate my priorities, my strengths, and my effectiveness. I realized that making appointments back to back all over town was not only unreasonable, it was foolish.

The word *harried* described me perfectly. I was distracted and less efficient due to the unyielding pace that left me unable to concentrate on the appointment or issue at hand. I was too busy trying to prepare for or make it to the next event. Have you ever talked with a person at a party who is constantly glancing over your shoulder looking for the next listener? This rude behavior leaves you feeling overlooked and ignored.

In the same way, when we scurry from one appointment to another, those we're interacting with can't help sensing our lack of attentiveness as we anticipate our next meeting. Maybe even more important, we lose the ability to enjoy the moment. We shortchange the other individuals and ourselves in the process. We lose the richness of life.

Now I try not to schedule more than one important appointment in each four- to five-hour block of the day. I consider my day in morning, afternoon, and evening blocks. I highlight one major focus in each block, whether a project, conversation, appointment, or meeting.

Do I do other things during that period? Yes. I may make phone calls, complete paperwork, or work on other lower priority items, but no more than one major priority item retains my concentration.

I can't even describe all the benefits of this new approach. My life is immeasurably enhanced.

Step 2: Recognize your responses of resistance to chaos and face the truth. The changes I've just described were very hard to make. It felt like I *ought* to be pushing myself, working harder rather than relaxing in my approach. I feared that my effectiveness, ability to produce, and accomplishment would be reduced, or that I wouldn't be as sharp in my thinking.

Ironically, the opposite occurred. My thinking cleared and became more organized, making me more effective. In each day, I actually got more done, and it was better-quality work because I paid more attention to details. My conversations with friends and family were enhanced. My memory was more exact. The value of allowing time for chaos amazed me. My stress lessened, and I was more relaxed.

Yet my resistance systems often rose up in revolt. I continued to be tempted to structure the chaos out of my life, falling back into the old systems that left me rushed and harried. I missed the adrenaline high of busyness. I sometimes reverted to snapping quick responses to people who interrupted me with phone calls.

Those telephone calls became a gauge, reminding me when I was resisting the chaos again, overstructuring my life. Was I embracing the chaos, allowing it to weave into the fabric of my life, or was I still resisting it, pronouncing it a nuisance and a bother?

Step 3: Abandon your faulty systems for chaos management. When I realized my resistance systems were rearing their ugly heads again, I would make an effort to give them up, to yield to the Divine Designer and his orchestration of life. I would remind myself that there are only twenty-four hours in each day—whatever I accomplished in my waking hours would have to be enough for that day.

The work wouldn't disappear. If it was important, I would tackle it the next day. If it wasn't, I would either ignore it or include it in a future focus. My life became characterized by the words of Jesus Christ, "Therefore do not worry about tomorrow, for tomorrow will worry about itself. Each day has enough trouble of its own."[4] An excellent guideline for life.

Step 4: Discover peace in life's process. When you consider the eternal scheme of things, we do a lot of things each day that don't matter much. But the Divine Orchestrator takes our daily offerings and weaves them together into his pattern. He knows us better than we know ourselves, understands our weaknesses, and imparts far more mercy than we ever allow ourselves.

With this in mind, I can give new energy to every moment, because I know that each moment counts. Rather than considering only incidents *I* consider important, moving from one urgent need to the next, I can now value every moment and every incident, no matter how trivial it may seem. *Why is this significant in the grand scheme of things?* I wonder, as new events unfold. I am discovering a new peace in this process.

Step 5: Let go of your control. Now what happens when the telephone rings? Well, I must admit my first inclination is still to view it as an interruption—but then I take a deep breath, clear my thoughts, and reach for the receiver. I give the caller my complete attention by relaxing and willingly engaging in the conversation. This is no interruption; it's a divine appointment.

In this way, I give up control of each event. Soon the whole day is out of my control—and in God's. I can trust this Superforce, the Divine Orchestrator and Conductor. He knows very well what he's doing. If I yield to him and his plans, then his best plan for this one day of my existence on earth will be fulfilled.

Continuing Steps in the Journey

That sounds very nice, you may be saying, but what if you've got a million things to do and the friend on the phone just wants to chat? Certainly some interruptions are more urgent than others, as we see in the next step of the Chaos Factor, which is to evaluate the options, make choices, and integrate the chaos.

Step 6: Evaluate the options, make choices, and integrate the chaos.

When someone calls, I have several options. If I have time constraints at that point, I quickly evaluate the nature of the call, determining whether I need to dismiss it (a salesperson), postpone it (a friend who wants to chat), or take time with it (an urgent need). I ask any questions that will help me judge the situation, and if I need to postpone the issue, I simply explain my time crunch. Most people are considerate. They'll excuse themselves and wait for a later conversation. If they continue to talk, apparently unable to hang up the phone, then I know their need is greater than my schedule.

At this point, I forget everything else and listen. I yield to the Divine Orchestrator. I put my schedule on hold. I give the caller my complete attention, trusting that my schedule will yield to the Divine Orchestrator's hand. He will bring order to the remaining events of the day. Sometimes the plans on my agenda never take place. That's when I know my agenda wasn't as important as God's. Other times, supernatural occurrences happen.

Often, I find I am able to complete twice the work in an allotted period than I imagined possible. Or someone volunteers to complete a task on my agenda. Or the task becomes no longer necessary. I believe these amazing occurrences are happening all around us every day as God, by his Spirit, faithfully accomplishes his will, shifting our plans to accommodate his.

But how do you evaluate your options? How do you know whether the interruption is worth taking time for? Or what if it's not just a phone call, but some chaotic event that throws off your plans? What if it's a matter of marriage or divorce, injury or disease, getting or losing a job, making a move to a different state or country? Those big events always present you with choices to evaluate and make, as you integrate into your life the chaos God is sending your way.

Choices

So let's talk about choices. They shape our lives, but as you know, they're often difficult to make. Because of life's ambiguity, we may be faced simultaneously with several possibilities of comparable value. If every choice were between good and bad, it would be easy. But most of our choices involve good and also good—or bad and maybe not quite as bad. Choosing one over another is tough.

If a woman is choosing a man to marry, she may find several suitable individuals who have different characteristics. How can she know which one to choose? She can make lists of qualities and lists of problems and try to reason it all out, but who can reason in matters of the heart?

Yet we might say that any decision we have to make is—to some extent—a matter of the heart. One author writes, "In important human problems, there is no such thing as making a logical decision in the midst of chaos. One uses the resources at hand (feeling, conscious and unconscious knowledge, hereditary information and so forth) to arrive at a decision—a preference."[5] And who's to say, even after applying all these resources, that our choice is right?

I talked with Nathaniel, a graduating high school senior, about the process of choosing a college to attend.

"I'm really not sure yet," he said. "I've been accepted at three. One may offer me a soccer scholarship. One may let me play football, which I love best. And the other is a Christian college offering me training I wouldn't be able to find elsewhere. The academics are great at all of them."

"So what do you think?" I asked.

"Oh, I don't know. I just can't decide. My parents graduated from the one where I could play football. They loved it there. But the scholarship would sure be terrific at the other school. And I may decide to be involved in Christian education. I'd need the training offered by the third."

Nathaniel offered point after logical point to evaluate each school. But every time he seemed to lean toward one over the others, he thought of other considerations. When it came time for Nathaniel to leave, I realized he was no closer to a decision than when he began.

A month later I saw one of his friends, and I asked what Nathaniel had finally decided. The friend laughed, "You won't believe it. Nathaniel paid a deposit to all three schools to hold his place for the fall. He's still not sure where to go."

I was thoroughly familiar with Nathaniel's dilemma. I watched my daughter debate the same points and take the same action last year before she finally decided to attend the University of North Carolina at Chapel Hill. The decision-making process became such a problem that my usually congenial daughter would become angry when anyone asked where she planned to go. "Don't ask me," she'd snap. "I don't know and I don't want to talk about it. I'll tell you when I get there."

Guidelines for the Process

So how do we make satisfactory choices? I believe these guidelines will prove helpful.

1. Gather information. You can't make intelligent judgments without the facts. "In some cases, gaining information may require a lot of asking, listening, remembering, imagining, and getting advice from knowledgeable people."[6] Certainly the Bible, as our instruction book for life, can aid in our decision-making, too, as it gives us a sense of God's priorities.

2. *Evaluate the alternatives.* Having gathered all the facts you can find, look at your alternatives. Apply the journalistic questions so familiar to any newsperson: who, what, where, when, why, and how? What other choices can be made? What are the benefits and drawbacks of each choice? What will be the consequences? Who will object? Where may a particular choice lead?

Though sometimes inconclusive, the process of evaluating the options is still very important. God has given us internal resources to aid us in eliminating options that aren't beneficial. In essence, we tune out the noise from the music of life. Options can be evaluated by listing the pros and cons, the expected good and bad results, the repercussions of one choice over another. As you evaluate each decision, imagine how the picture of your future would change for each course you might choose.

For example, I am now considering a career change. My successful career as a writer, speaker, and broadcaster seems too predictable. I want to consider new challenges, take new risks, and broaden my interests and expertise. I have considered several positions in which I would use my skills and abilities in different ways. Considering these opportunities, I find myself imagining, *What would it be like to live in this or that part of the country, to work in that environment, to fulfill those responsibilities?* In this way, I've ruled out several prospects, realizing that I'm uncomfortable with some potential aspects of the imagined picture.

But as diligently as you study the choices, there will still be things you don't know about them. Chaos demands that we factor mystery into the equation. That can be difficult for those of us who want to be one hundred percent certain about everything. How can you make a choice that may radically change your life without *knowing* how it will turn out?

As I contemplate a career change, I know I'll be meeting a different set of people. My children's lives will also be changed because of a different community environment, a new school system, and other factors. The fact is that I have no idea what all the repercussions of my decision will be, so I must embrace God, chaos, mystery, and the unfolding process of life.

3. Make a choice. Having gathered and evaluated the information, make a choice. If you deliberate forever, indecision becomes your choice. Sometimes you just need to step out in darkness, take the risk, and trust the Divine Orchestrator to work his wonders in his mysterious ways.

This may make you feel uncomfortable. As author Leonard Foley describes the experience, "Now more reality sets in: You're not absolutely certain. . . . You're afraid. . . . It's a risk. . . . Welcome to the club!"

That's right. We all have to take those risks. "No concrete decision will automatically turn out to be as 'correct' as you hoped," Foley continues. *"Every decision is a risk,* even the most prudent one."[7]

4. Just do it. Nike's now famous slogan, "Just Do It," captures the next step in decision-making. You need to act on your choice. You may have chosen to tell someone how you really feel about him or her—or to remain silent. Regardless, having made the choice, act on it. It's the only way to move forward.

So you've encountered a bit of chaos. Some interruption has broken into your life, presenting you with choices, perhaps major ones. After evaluating the options, you make a choice and act on it. In this whole process, you are embracing chaos rather than resisting it. The melody of chaos is integrated into the symphony of your life.

But now you need to face another fascinating element of the Chaos Factor: *There is no turning back.* If that statement leaves a scary, empty feeling in the pit of your stomach, you're not alone. Most of us respond with terror to the "no turning back" reality of life. We realize that our choices do make a difference and the difference is irrevocable.

Does this mean you can never correct mistakes, fix what needs repair, or change a faulty choice? Absolutely not. But there is no aspect of the past that can be blotted out as if it never had occurred.

Integrating Daily Chaos into the Fabric of Life

Whatever your choices, they contributed to your present circumstances, permanently affected the flow of your life, and left you with only the option to move forward. All of life moves steadily toward a new future. We live always on the brink of discovery.

The Irreversibility of Time

As scientists continue their studies about chaos, they have come to realize that every change made in any system is permanent. This precipitates other chaotic alterations that cannot be undone. Too many irrevocable changes have taken place.

For example, when a scientist conducts an experiment, there is never another time when it can be perfectly duplicated. Chaos ensures that. Something, if merely the date, will have changed and cannot be recaptured. Reversibility is an illusion. Prigogene, regarded as the father of chaos theory, states, "There are no reversible experiments. Therefore, our world is temporarily organized. There is always an arrow to time."[8]

What does this have to do with us? It further shows the importance of our choices as time moves forward, chaos is embraced, and our lives unfold. At the same time, it emphasizes the fact that new choices always give opportunity to new life in the midst of chaos.

Consider the Butterfly Effect. Small changes in a system are amplified by the changes they cause, making an impact of incalculable significance on the future. The single butterfly has knocked over a domino that sends the whole earth reeling. The butterfly cannot "unflap" its wings. As scientists describe it, there are many possible futures at any given point. But once made, a choice affects the whole system. "One future was chosen and the other possibilities vanished forever."[9]

Changes like that are happening every moment. We cannot undo anything, but we can make new choices that will have new effects.

Chaos Theory and Your Life

You can see the effects that your choices have on your life and the people around you. This can be sobering when you realize you can't undo your choices—but it doesn't have to be paralyzing. God is always working with your choices. He participates in the affairs of his creation as it moves forward in time. He is constantly crafting a new order, a new design for his creation, a future that's different from the past.

As you deal with chaos each day, remember that a new and beautiful tomorrow awaits. God's compassions, the Bible says, are "new every morning."[10] In Isaiah, God says, "Forget the former things; do not dwell on the past. See, I am doing a new thing! Now it springs up; do you not perceive it?"[11]

What is the new thing God is doing in your life as you walk this journey through chaos? Do you perceive it? The next time chaos hits, take heart.

I saw a clever greeting card that may describe the way you feel. A woman leans on one elbow at the kitchen table, empty coffee cup in front of her, lips pursed in displeasure. "I've been evaluating my life lately," she remarks, "and something tells me . . ." I opened the card and read, ". . . I should have picked door number 3." Ever feel that way? Well, even if you fear that your past choices have harmed you, there's still hope. You can make new choices, starting today, as you launch into the rest of your life. Embrace the chaotic interventions of life and embrace a new beginning each day, each moment. Take door number 4, number 5, number 6. Your future will never be the same again.

Integrating Traumatic Chaos into the Fabric of Life

The dance of life finds its beginnings in grief. . . . Here a completely new way of living is revealed. It is the way in which pain can be embraced, not out of a desire to suffer, but in the knowledge that something new will be born in the pain.

Henri Nouwen

The pungent odor of antiseptic permeated the office. Silver instruments lay neatly on a white cloth, glistening against the white walls, white smocks, and white cabinets of the sterile examining room. Suddenly the walls seemed to be coming closer, closing in on me. Cuddling my new-born in the crook of my arm, I stared in disbelief at the doctor. Surely, he's wrong. Surely, there's some mistake. My mind frantically searched for explanations. Silence prevailed.

Only six weeks earlier I'd suffered the trauma of an unexpected caesarean section. Twelve weeks earlier, my parents' minister in Florida had called to break the news that my father had set out on his routine morning walk only to fall dead of a massive heart attack. Now this doctor was giving me numbing test results: I had Hodgkin's disease.

It was unreal. A dream. It couldn't be true.

During a regular pregnancy checkup and sonogram months before, the attending physician had noticed my greatly enlarged spleen. He made no comment at the time. For fear of disrupting my pregnancy, the group of attending physicians decided not to mention it until after the birth. The anticipated six-week checkup provided the opportunity to give me this news.

I was shocked. I left the office in a daze and returned home feeling as though my world had caved in. The tears wouldn't stop. Now what?

When the Dam Breaks

What do you do after your tears run dry and the harsh reality of chaos remains? What do you do next? How do you deal with the suffering?

In this chapter we'll apply the truths we've learned about the Chaos Factor to the traumas of life. How do you respond to the chaos of life's traumas? How can you respond more effectively?

My diagnosis delivered, the doctor's responsibility satisfied, now the journey through chaos began. The steps of the Chaos Factor were in motion.

Step 1: Acknowledge that chaos is the raw material of life. I remember rocking my sleeping baby, thinking that the thing I feared most had come upon me. Cancer. The dread disease that was stealing more and more lives. I thought it could never happen to me. Heart attack? Yes. Almost all relatives on both sides of my family died of heart attacks . . . but cancer? No. Yet the unimaginable had happened.

Then I asked all the usual rhetorical questions. I probably spent weeks subconsciously asking them. *Why me? Why now? How could this have happened to me?* Yet I found no answers.

I've come to realize that God rarely answers the why questions, at least not at the moment they're asked. He usually responds with "Trust me." We see this throughout the Bible. We need to allow time for the process to unfold. Later, looking back, we may see more clearly, but not when the questions first arise. So I finally stopped asking why. It seemed meaningless, unproductive.

Then I wondered about other people who were grappling with the reality of cancer. I began to consider the survivors. I reminded myself that it was possible to survive cancer.

This is what helped me accept the chaos as I adjusted to the ramifications of what the doctor had told me: *It's happened to others. It happens every day. There are survivors.*

Step 2: Recognize your responses of resistance to chaos and face the truth. How did I resist the chaos? My first response was blindness. I sat in the doctor's office assuming that it was simply a mistake. Even after accepting the news, there were times I wanted to believe it wasn't true.

My next response was to busy myself with family responsibilities. I tried to structure everything. Because the future was out of control, I tried to exert control over the present—every minute, hour, and day. To control my emotions, I began acting like a robot as I carried out everyday activities. As I denied my feelings, my voice began to sound like that of a Marine sergeant: dispassionate, expressionless, in control.

Step 3: Abandon your faulty systems for chaos management. After beginning to hate the sound of my voice and the numbness in my heart, I finally grieved. I sorrowed over the fact that these coping mechanisms weren't working. I lamented that I might not have a future, that I might never see my children grow up. I felt the pain of disillusionment and dashed hopes. I allowed myself to face my situation and mourn.

Step 4: Discover peace in life's process. Then I began to alter my perspective. Since my days probably were numbered (though I didn't know *what* number), I figured I'd simply enjoy each day to the fullest. I would abandon the driving busyness of extraneous activity and invest my remaining days in my family. I would develop a new serenity. I knew the process would simply unfold and I would flow with its turns and twists like a leaf floating down a meandering stream. I would gain courage in taking one day at a time while trusting God to orchestrate the process as he chose.

And so I resigned from committees, canceled appointments, and determinedly learned to say no when no was appropriate. After all, Jesus Christ, who touched comparatively few lives while he walked this earth, was able to tell God, "Father, I have brought you glory on earth by completing the work you gave me to do."[1] It became my goal to fulfill my God-given destiny for the time that remained.

Step 5: Let go of your control. I began to hold all of life loosely. I never knew if I had tomorrow, so I appreciated each day. I learned to be a facilitator in the lives of my family and others rather than a controller. I stopped being in charge. I gave up scores of leadership positions, choosing instead the role of cheerleader and mentor, counselor and friend. Growing dependence on me would cripple rather than strengthen everyone I was associated with, so I encouraged them to place their dependence on the only person who would not change and who would be there when I couldn't be. I placed my dependence on this Creator God, too.

Step 6: Evaluate the options, make choices, and integrate the chaos. When your life has a deadline (in an all-too-literal sense of the word), your time becomes precious to you. Choosing how to spend it becomes even more important. I changed the way I related to people. They weren't interruptions anymore; they were God-given opportunities. Having come face to face with chaos, I was incorporating it into the flow as my life moved forward into its mysterious future.

Then a remarkable thing happened. The doctor called me into his office, apologized, announced that the Hodgkin's disease was a misdiagnosis, and sent me home with a clean bill of health. Talk about shock! I only *thought* I had been shocked by his first diagnosis. Now I was stunned speechless. By that time, however, the integration of the chaos was so complete I couldn't imagine living any other way. The Chaos Factor had changed my life and there was no going back, nor did I want there to be.

In the last chapter, I discussed the irreversibility of time. In this case, it *seemed* as though something had been reversed. My death sentence had been revoked. But I'm convinced it was all part of a forward-moving plan. The choices I made when I thought I was dying have changed my life forever. Time and chaos have moved on, and I've moved with them—no bitterness, no sadness, no regret.

Experiences Illustrate the Chaos Factor

I have gathered the stories of others to demonstrate the six steps of the Chaos Factor in the traumatic events of life, because I think they'll help you deal with whatever chaos you're facing. I want you to become a chaos survivor instead of a chaos statistic.

I met Patricia while teaching a course in my community titled "Living in the Midst of Chaos." Blond, in her mid-thirties, Patricia came with troubled eyes to greet me after her first time in attendance. "I so appreciated your presentation. But I can't seem to grasp the real impact of what you're saying about chaos. I'm struggling in my own life right now, finding it almost impossible to make sense out of it. I almost committed suicide lately, and I'm trying to get help. I can tell that what you're saying is true. Somehow I believe there is a God orchestrating all of life's chaos—I wouldn't be alive otherwise. But I can't understand how to make sense of it all."

Through the next weeks I noticed that Patricia's expressions changed. The consternation in her eyes seemed to clear. A smile began to touch her lips. She seemed brighter, happier, and more able to cope.

When the session was finished, she handed me this poem to explain all that she was attempting to assimilate and her conclusions about the pervasive nature of the chaos in her life. She gave me permission to share it with you, and I count it a privilege.

Ashes of Beauty
Heavenly Father hear my plea;
My life is in shambles
From what the world has done to me;
Pain from the loss of innocence as a child;
Discounted feelings; from hearing they are friends
    quiet it will be.
Loss of trust in the family—where can a child go?
No love spoken in this home;
Continued abuse—nowhere to go;
Anger and yelling—curling up in fear,
A body changing—drawing attention,
Bad choices from no direction.
Where does a growing child go?
Depression, low self-esteem, thoughts of death;
Where does a young adult go?
Bad choices, bad relationships,

Is abuse all she'll know?
Death comes emotionally—
Thoughts about God . . . Why didn't you stop it?
What's wrong with me?
Plans for death by suicide;
Hospitalization, therapy, choices, forgiving, acceptance;
Accepting that Christ died for me He loved me so.
Teach me more God, as I begin again;
Delivered from death unto life
As the ashes of my past are . . .
Reaching out in the beauty of your love
To help others find the beauty of life
    Amongst the ashes.

                                          Patricia James

Integrating Traumatic Chaos into the Fabric of Life

This poignant poem portrays the confusion of suffering at the hands of a chaos-filled world. Why all this suffering? Where does the pain come from?

In the midst of chaos, it seems there are at least four causes of suffering.

1. We live in a broken world. Our ancient ancestors rebelled against God's plan in Eden's paradise and a fallen, broken world was the consequence. Scientists call this brokenness *entropy*—the continuous, unavoidable process of deterioration, the slowing down of life through a loss of energy. People age, matter deteriorates, as entropy has its way. Like a butterfly flapping its wings, the original sin in Eden sent its effects reverberating through the universe, causing broken people, broken dreams, broken ideals.

2. We make poor choices. Every choice carries a consequence; sometimes this can be extremely painful. Stolen love, violent revenge, passive deceit . . . the list goes on. We often cause our own suffering.

3. God sometimes sends suffering to protect us. The sensation of physical pain, for instance, is a valuable gift. It often tells us when we're in danger. Sometimes God has an ultimately merciful plan that requires some pain along the way. Imagine a frightened teenager named Mary suffering birth pangs while bearing the Christ child. It hurt for a time, but in the long run it was worth it. We usually grow through such difficult experiences.

4. We may suffer abuse from others because we trust Christ. The apostle Paul knew this suffering well.

> "People are watching us as we stay at our post," he wrote, "alertly, unswervingly . . . in hard times, tough times, bad times; when we're beaten up, jailed, and mobbed; working hard, working late, working without eating; with pure heart, clear head, steady hand; in gentleness, holiness, and honest love; when we're telling the truth, and when God's showing his power; when we're doing our best setting things right; when we're praised, and when we're blamed; slandered, and honored; true to our word, though distrusted; ignored by the world, but recognized by God; terrifically

141

Embracing the Chaos

alive, though rumored to be dead; beaten within an inch of our lives, but refusing to die; immersed in tears, yet always filled with deep joy; living on handouts, yet enriching many; having nothing, having it all."[2]

Martyrs throughout the ages have known this suffering. In the second century, the aged Bishop Polycarp was arrested for being a Christian and forced to stand in the arena with thousands calling for his murder. The Roman proconsul shouted, "Swear and I will release you. Curse the Christ and you will live." Polycarp lifted his head, looked at his accusers, and said, "Eighty-six years I have served Him and He has done me no wrong. How can I blaspheme my King who saved me?" Polycarp was martyred that day.

Sometimes Christians are called to suffer for the God who transcends suffering.

Suffering is a real part of the chaos, yet hope remains as the strains of the great symphony of life rise and fall with the Conductor's gentle hand. On the top of a marble statue found in Broyhill Park in Blowing Rock, North Carolina, sits a weathered anvil. Inscribed on the bronze plaque at its side are the words of J. E. Broyhill, "God forges us on an anvil of adversity for a purpose known only to Him. This is how He prepares us for life."

Having looked at suffering, let's hear the true stories of others as the Chaos Factor applies to their lives.

Step 1: Acknowledge That Chaos Is the Raw Material of Life

T. R. left her brother-in-law's home in Knoxville, Tennessee, at about four in the morning. Her husband, John, hadn't driven far before the fog was so dense that only the taillights ahead showed the road. Tense and alarmed, they drove in silence.

Soon after daybreak, they saw a hitchhiker ahead and debated whether to pick him up. Though T. R. reminded John of the dangers, he stopped anyway.

The young man turned out to be harmless and entertaining, relating many adventures he'd experienced as he traveled across the country. They stopped for breakfast and were returning to the car when he said, "I noticed a sign pointing in the direction of West Virginia. I think I'll get out here and continue on my way." John and T. R. were disappointed to say good-bye, but God apparently had other plans . . . for all of them.

It was dusk when it happened. T. R. and John were traveling through the mountains on Route 11 near Lexington, Virginia, at a leisurely pace, expecting to arrive at their northern Virginia home in late evening. They were approaching the crest of a hill when they met a large tractor-trailer heading their way in their lane of traffic. John tried to avoid a head-on collision by pulling onto the shoulder of the road. Unfortunately, the truck driver made the same move.

They were dragged ninety yards down the mountain. At that moment a news photographer was heading home from work. He caught the accident on film—the demolished small car and the position of the truck. Unconscious and dying, John and T. R. were taken to a small country hospital. T. R. was bleeding profusely from a head injury and needed an immediate blood transfusion. But T. R. had fairly rare B-negative blood, and the doctors could find only one donor in the vicinity with type-B blood—they didn't check whether it was positive or negative. They went ahead with the transfusion and later learned the donor's blood was positive, not a match.

This transfusion continued to cause health problems for T. R. over the next few years. Four weeks after the accident, she returned home by ambulance, but was still bed-ridden.

When T. R.'s first child, a daughter, was born, the baby was extremely jaundiced and the pathologist was uncertain whether she would survive. Doctors had to perform a blood exchange transfusion, the first ever done on a baby in that hospital. After that traumatic beginning, the baby not only survived but has become a living testimony to God's intervention in sustaining life.

But that isn't the end of the story. T. R. had a son, too, born at eight months by caesarean section. During this pregnancy, an obstetrician and a pathologist studied T. R.'s case to learn more about how to assure babies would survive such circumstances. T. R.'s son did need a transfusion, but he survived and grew up to be a family physician.

Yet another good thing came out of this accident. John and T. R. had seldom attended church, but the accident jolted them into realizing something was missing from their lives—God. They became active members of a vibrant church, rearing their children to love God and cherish his gifts.

Every so often T. R. wonders what became of that hitchhiker. His destiny was also determined that day when he decided *not* to continue on that journey with them. The chaos that changed everything for John and T. R. was not a part of life's plan for him. Do you wonder what was?

Integrating the chaos of a tragic accident, T. R. and her husband found their lives permanently altered. Rather than becoming bitter over an event that could have been misconstrued as a cruel twist of fate, they took a positive turn toward God that shaped their lives forever.

Step 2: Recognize Your Responses of Resistance to Chaos and Face the Truth

Karin was involved with a mission church project in Pennsylvania. A small group met for Bible study, seeking to do God's will in planting a new church. Eight years later, they were holding hands and singing "Blessed Be the Tie That Binds," as they closed the doors of the church for the last time.

During those eight years, they saw several hundred people come and go through its doors. Several pastors, church leaders, choirs, and committees came and went. It was a church with afflictions from the beginning: a lack of denominational support, conflict with leadership, too many visionaries.

However, it was also a haven for churchgoers who didn't fit anywhere else. Many people who would not have considered leadership elsewhere felt safe in trying it at this young church. Musicians who never dared to sing a solo elsewhere took a risk among this small group of close friends. Leaders were born, young believers grew in their knowledge of God and Bible, and many, like Karin, who thought they understood God's will, learned some new lessons.

The church was closed when the leaders decided it could not maintain the pastor's salary. Rather than creating hurt feelings with people leaving bit by bit, the leaders agreed to allow the church to die. People die, churches die—this is sometimes God's will. For Karin, it felt as though a large part of her family had died. Many of the people grieved for a year or more.

"But we all learned many things," Karin says now. "We learned that what is extremely painful now can and does bring forth new growth later. Reflecting on the good that came out of what many misunderstood as a failure, we learned there are no failures when you set out to do God's will! Doing God's will may mean not looking so successful to others. Success is measured by God's ruler, his standard alone."

Karin and the other members chose not to use their own systems of resistance to force the continuation of their church. Instead, they abandoned their coping mechanisms, chose not to yield to peer pressure that might whisper failure and defeat, and allowed God's orchestration of the chaos to guide them. Although this was painful, it brought each of them to a new place of understanding and growth.

Giving up our coping mechanisms and choosing to accept the chaos often transforms tragedy into a blessing in disguise. Faced with a similar tragedy, another friend wrote, "In my own experience, when chaos was at its devastating worst, I was *least* capable of handling it. Perhaps that was why it *was* chaos. My biggest mistake was trying to handle it in my own strength, which resulted in digging myself deeper while frantically trying to escape. It was not until I totally gave up and trusted God enough to tell him, 'Do whatever it takes,' that a ray of light broke through, and I started learning to cope. It was the turning point in my life."

And the results prove something else about chaos. Each incident I've mentioned has involved benefits. Have you ever thought that some of the chaos in your life might benefit someone else? Through Karin's church, lives were enriched and new growth was begun, not only in their lives but in the life of every person touched by their chaos.

I found an insightful passage about hope and growth through suffering in the novel *A Wolf Story,* by J. Huggins.

> "The Lightmaker is always with you," Saul said gently. "But our hearts are filled with many things, so we don't hear him. That's why so often it's only in times of suffering that we finally understand, because it is then we finally listen. And then we come to know his love for us. We become one with the Lightmaker, and strength comes for the task.
>
> "Don't feel that you are alone. Everyone must endure . . . the Dark Night of the Soul. Sometimes it lasts for days. Sometimes it lasts for years. But it is something we must all endure, to find our strength. There is no shame in your pain. It only means that the Lightmaker is working within you, burning away everything that makes you weak. Don't run from the pain. Embrace it bravely, and look into your heart. Then allow the Lightmaker to destroy within you all those things that keep you from him. The pain is great, but in the end, if you will only endure, you will stand in new strength and a new life."[3]

Step 3: Abandon Your Faulty Systems for Chaos Management

Shirley, a medical transcriptionist, was suddenly told her office was being shut down. She would be paid for only two more weeks. Now fifty years old, divorced, and with a mortgage to pay, Shirley had worked full-time in this profession for almost two decades. It didn't occur to her to take advantage of unemployment compensation, so she watched the classified ads and took the first medical transcription job she saw advertised.

She went to work for a radiology group of physicians in a small town, taking a large cut in pay and benefits. She had to type her transcriptions on a typewriter rather than into a computer, as she was accustomed. Since she was now transcribing only X-rays, living in a small town, and unable to use advanced equipment, she feared losing the advanced skills she had developed. But a job was a job.

Shirley's office was a storage room. The phone sat on the floor. She kept searching for another position for the two years she worked there. "I hated the job," she said later, "and I couldn't understand why God had put me there. I got to the point where I hated it so much and was under so much stress I considered quitting without first finding another job."

But then she heard through unusual circumstances (from someone in a distant city) that a company in her home state was looking for home transcriptionists. She had never considered this because she assumed the pay and benefits would be dismal, but she decided to look into it. The company took one look at all her experience and practically hired her on the spot. She took the job, trusting God to provide for her needs. It has turned out to be the highest paying job she's ever had.

"God put me in a situation that I would hate enough to be willing to take a risk that I had previously been unwilling to take," she says now as she looks back on it. "Also, working for that radiology service made me much more valuable to my current employer, because they find it difficult to find general medical transcriptionists who can transcribe radiology reports."

Shirley's story confirms statements I've heard many times. Not only do the chaotic traumas in our lives often bring about a brighter future, but the very thing we hate is often the thing that makes it work. I've created a contemporary proverb that proves true time and again: There's no waste in God's economy. The parts of our lives that we're desperate to avoid or escape often become essential elements of our future success.

Think back over some negative experience in your life. Can you, like Shirley, recognize an unexpected benefit in it? Maybe LifeMapping will help you.

LifeMapping is an evaluative technique developed by author and counselor John Trent. He writes, "Fifteen years ago I learned how to 'storyboard' from a person who headed Disney's 'think tank.' When Walt Disney made his first cartoon back in the 1920's, he drew little sketches on paper to break down the production of *Steamboat Willie* into manageable parts. With LifeMapping I teach people how to storyboard the key aspects of their lives so they can see the twists and turns they have taken—and where they got stuck. Without storyboarding, looking back can get pretty complicated, particularly if you're getting older and have a lot of history to cover."[4]

In storyboarding, you "picture" your life by posting everything that's happened to you—the good and bad, personal triumphs and deferred dreams. It enables you to see God's process unfolding throughout your life. This view of your past gives you a picture of who you are, how you have changed in attitudes and beliefs, and who you can be. It provides a goal so you will become a better person. It enables you to examine your choices and make similar or different ones in the future based on their success or failure. It helps you see where your growth has been hindered or stopped.

Trent divides life into four categories: strengths, freeze points, flash points, and major transitions. You plot these by noting how you've responded to chaos. As you see God's positive integration of the chaos of your past, you can begin to plot a positive future.

The Israelites were instructed by God to create a record of his faithful actions in their lives. In the same way, we can find confidence to go forward as we look back at God's faithfulness throughout our past.

What are your God-given strengths? To understand them, you need to see how your gifts, talents, and abilities have developed—often being tested in crisis situations.

What are your freeze points? These are the seasons of life that leave us emotionally frozen, perhaps the events of a tough childhood, for example. As we look at them with insight and realize that they hold no power over us, we see them as blended fibers in the tapestry of life. We can then choose to grieve over them, but then move on to a hopeful future.

What are your flash points? These are the incidents on your LifeMap that positively or negatively changed the course of your life. The apostle Paul met the ascended Jesus as he traveled to Damascus to arrest Christians.[5] This dramatic encounter would constitute a flash point—a permanent and irrevocable change of direction that shaped the rest of his life. Your flash points may not be quite as miraculous (though they could be), but they will be your most significant moments of decision and change.

And finally, what are your major transitions? Trent writes, "Here we look back and ask, 'What are the key transitions we were forced to make?' I know one woman who has moved twenty-two times with her corporate husband. That's a lot of transition. But just getting married and having kids are huge transitions."[6]

LifeMapping gives us perspective. It helps us relax in the process of chaos and trust the God of the process. It also helps us move beyond the difficult periods of our lives. In *Here and Now,* Henri Nouwen speaks of the value of God's process:

> But understanding our wounds is not enough. Finally we must find freedom to step over our wounds and the courage to forgive those who have wounded us. The real danger is to get stuck in anger and resentment. Then we start living as the "wounded one," always complaining that life isn't "fair."
>
> Jesus came to save us from those self-destructive complaints. He says, "Let go of your complaints, forgive those who loved you

poorly, step over your feelings of being rejected, and have courage to trust that you won't fall into an abyss of nothingness but into the safe embrace of a God whose love will heal all your wounds."[7]

Step 4: Discover Peace in Life's Process

Caryl and her husband decided to sell their small but comfortable ranch house to buy something bigger and better. The deal fell through after they closed on their old house, so they wound up renting a townhouse. They kept looking for "something better."

That's when they started attending their present church. In one sermon the pastor challenged the people to adopt the biblical practice of tithing (giving God ten percent of their income). He even offered a money-back guarantee! They could try tithing for three to six months, and if it created a financial hardship for them, they could ask the church leaders for their money back.

Up to this point, Caryl and her husband had assumed they couldn't afford to tithe. They gave *some* to the church, but ten percent? They had enough financial problems already. But the pastor's challenge inspired them, and they decided to try it.

How did it work out? "Well," Caryl says, "not only did it not create a hardship, but we have been blessed in so many ways, most significantly with changed hearts. We now give our financial tithe happily, even joyfully, and we have a greater sense of peace and contentment than we've ever known. This doesn't mean we got the 'bigger, better house' we used to want. Because our hearts are in a different place, we were content to move into a mobile home left to us by my husband's mother. It is big enough to meet our family's needs, affordable for us, and it allowed us to stay in the same town where my children attend school. What a blessing!

"We also learned that when you trust God, things happen—like changed hearts. In addition, we discovered there's a big difference between what we want and what we need. God is faithful, and when we want his way, he provides our needs and blessings besides."

Sometimes chaos changes the way we think. Things we thought were important lose their value, and things that previously seemed to have little significance prove to be most important. Caryl's story demonstrates the value of giving up control and letting go of things we think we want, opening ourselves to other perspectives. Step 5 of the Chaos Factor, relinquishing control, teaches us new things about ourselves and about life that we might not otherwise learn.

Step 5: Let Go of Your Control

Tony and his wife were struggling in their marriage. The problems intensified until finally they agreed to attend a Marriage Encounter weekend recommended by some friends. The weekend didn't just patch up their marriage; it brought Tony's wife into a real relationship with God. Afterward, they found a new church to attend together, one that would help them grow in their faith. "This started a journey of healing in our marriage," Tony says. "Needless to say, this weekend dramatically changed our lives together."

Whether a tragic accident or the trauma of a troubled marriage, chaos can bring about positive conclusions. In the case of Tony and his wife, the pain of marital strife forced them to seek a change—more chaos, really. The Marriage Encounter weekend promised to shuffle around the ways they dealt with each other, but they knew they needed this. All attempts to ignore problems or structure them had failed. By seeking out this change agent—the conference—Tony and his wife were incorporating the reality of chaos into their lives. And their lives *were* changed, far more than they expected.

Stories like these demonstrate the effectiveness of the Chaos Factor in dealing with crises. Underlying each story is the presence of the Divine Orchestrator. As we face chaos, we are able to give up control with confidence by trusting in this God who is sovereign. If we begin to read the Bible in a new way, looking for the character qualities of this God, we make exciting discoveries. We learn that this all-powerful God is a:

Promise-keeper. "His divine power has given us everything we need for life and godliness through our knowledge of him who called us by his own glory and goodness. Through these he has given us his very great and precious promises, so that through them you may participate in the divine nature and escape the corruption in the world that is caused by evil desires."[8]

Faithful ruler. David says to God in prayer, "Who am I, O Sovereign LORD, and what is my family, that you have brought me this far? And as if this were not enough in your sight, O Sovereign LORD, you have also spoken about the future of the house of your servant. Is this your usual way of dealing with man, O Sovereign LORD? . . . How great you are, O Sovereign LORD! There is no one like you, and there is no God but you, as we have heard with our own ears."[9]

Tender caretaker. "See, the Sovereign LORD . . . tends his flock like a shepherd: He gathers the lambs in his arms and carries them close to his heart; he gently leads those that have young."[10]

Protector. "The Sovereign LORD has given me an instructed tongue, to know the word that sustains the weary. He wakens me morning by morning, wakens my ears to listen like one being taught. The Sovereign LORD has opened my ears, and I have not been rebellious; I have not drawn back. I offered my back to those who beat me, my cheeks to those who pulled out my beard; I did not hide my face from mocking and spitting. Because the Sovereign LORD helps me, I will not be disgraced. Therefore I have set my face like flint, and I know I will not be put to shame."[11]

Integrating Traumatic Chaos into the Fabric of Life

Step 6: Evaluate the Options, Make Choices, and Integrate the Chaos

I'd like to close this chapter with another of Patricia's poems. Written sometime after the first one, it demonstrates God's weaving of suffering and heartache into the golden tapestry of new life.

Weaving
O Lord, hear my prayer;
Take the threads of my life:
Weave them together into something beautiful;
From the blacks and grays of my past
Where there was nothingness and pain;
Weave in strength and patience.
As I strive to learn from them,
Weave in the glimpses of light that shone through,
Saying "Yes" there is more to life.
Weave bright colors;
Compassion, kindness, humility and gentleness;
Bind them all together with love:
A love that can only come from above,
Teaching wisdom through your word,
Weave in the peace that only Christ can bring
As He lives in me,
So that I may weave in from my heart
Songs and praises of gratitude
Through service to You, my Lord.

Patricia James

Ruth Myers has written the following prayer, expressing her attitude of thanksgiving for the chaotic crises of life—experiences that are transformed to enrich and enhance life.

Father, I am so delighted that You are both loving and Sovereign . . . so I thank you for each disturbing or humbling situation in my life, for each breaking or cleansing process You are allowing, for each problem or hindrance, for each thing that triggers in me anxiety or anger or pain.

And I thank you in advance for each disappointment, each demanding duty, each pressure, each interruption that may arise in the coming hours and days. In spite of what I think or feel when I get my eyes off You, I choose not to resist my trials as intruders, but to welcome them as friends.

Thank you that each difficulty is an opportunity to see You work . . . that in Your time You will bring me out to a place of abundance. I rejoice that You plan to enrich and beautify me through each problem, each conflict, each struggle . . . that through them you expose my weaknesses and needs, my hidden sins, my self-centeredness and especially my self-reliance and pride.

Thank you that You use trials to humble me and perfect my faith and produce in me the quality of endurance.[12]

10

Integrating Chaos through Change Management in the Workplace

I think leadership of communities and organizations is going to be about establishing a framework that will replace our old ideas about industrialism and provide a way for people to find greater meaning and purpose in their lives and in their work.

Kim McManus

The women *leaders in* our organization gathered around me. This was a group I had founded some years before. Centered in the conference room was the stately walnut table that dwarfed all other furniture, and each coworker sat in place enjoying the camaraderie. Animated conversation rose and fell.

I glanced at the faces. Did any of them know how much they really meant to me? The organization had begun seven years earlier with five of us who wanted to create a weekly lecture series to nurture women in the community. They asked me to act as lecturer and leader. I agreed to lecture but insisted that our leadership should be a team effort to bring this embryonic vision to reality. They agreed. The rest became history.

After three months of planning and publicity, we advertised the first morning meeting in newspapers and over the radio. Within a few weeks, our group had swelled to sixty-five, and by the time of this meeting seven years later, more than 350 women had participated in the program. Loneliness was banished and new friendships were forged, while the women were intellectually stimulated and spiritually enriched. Life changed for all of us as we watched this germ of an idea bend, twist, and expand to accommodate unexpected growth. The organization transformed itself with each new chaotic infusion.

The combined personalities of the richly diverse leadership team melded over time to create one of the most thriving organizations in our community. The twelve presently seated around the conference table represented a living organization—to all observers a successful, constantly expanding phenomenon.

Today we were gathered to hear unexpected news. Quieting their banter, I opened our meeting by highlighting the many ups and downs of our history. We all marveled at its success and the joy we had experienced throughout its growth. But on this day we reached a new plateau. Because of a management change in our sponsoring organization, we no longer had a sponsor or a meeting place.

The questions outnumbered the answers. Where would we meet? How would we manage costs now that sponsorship was removed? Were all necessary adjustments for the change simply too much to tackle? Should we close down our work? Had it served its purpose?

One person suggested we simply turn to prayer. We believed God had directed us at our inception and would guide us at this juncture. We stopped to pray. Then we began to identify the multiple problems, possible solutions and contributions each of us could make in contacting other key individuals, locating a new meeting space, finding a sponsoring group, and relocating our organization. I listened, offered my suggestions or responses, and waited. Over the following two months these leaders worked as a team not only to relocate the entire organization but also to respond to the new daily chaotic interruptions these multiple adjustments caused. When it was time for the fall lecture series, everything was in place and the program was ready for a new beginning. The organization's success continues to this day.

In this chapter we will discover how the Chaos Factor applies in every arena of life by supplying effective tools for change management. The Chaos Factor doesn't just apply to our personal lives; it works in the workplace as well.

Stress in the Workplace

Let's begin by looking at the escalation of stress in the workplace. Stress signals our resistance to chaos, its resultant change, and our inability to handle it effectively.

Change is everywhere, escalating at a rate beyond the imagination of previous generations. Change management is the essential key to the future in private and public life.

Dr. John H. Howard, a professor and management psychologist at the University of Western Ontario, has surveyed executives since 1971. He has identified several causes of stress problems. "Executive positions are stressful even in good times because they involve uncertainty, overwork, a feeling of helplessness and urgency. Because executives have to make decisions based on insufficient or inconclusive information even in prosperous times, uncertainty is a constant, but it has intensified because of downsizing. Even if they make the right decisions today, executives don't know if they will keep their jobs," Howard observes.[1]

The uncertainty of chaos typically results in unpredictability about future success or failure. This uncertainty is driving many executives to maintain seventy-hour work weeks to keep up with the competition.

It also appears that executives have insufficient leisure breaks between tasks. "In studying 300 managers at 12 major companies, a typical executive performed a different task every seven minutes," writes a researcher.[2] That means changing focus more than eight times an hour. As a result, more than half of those in high-stress positions suffer from physical or mental health problems that include exhaustion, headaches, and insomnia.

In the same way that the connective tissue warns of possible infection by becoming inflamed around a wound, stress is the emotional inflammation of the nervous system that warns us of possible harm to the system. Stress warns us that we are not handling life well.

We resist the onslaught of change in our jobs, through the various mechanisms already discussed. We turn a blind eye to increased workloads, insisting that we can handle it all with a few more hours on the job. Or we try to structure our schedules to get everything done—usually leaving out any hours for relaxation.

But resistance to this chaos is harming us. Rather than resisting it, we should be accepting the chaos and integrating it, watching it produce new and positive opportunities. Unfortunately, much of the business world is still locked in old management systems that resist change. These structures promote stress rather than relieve it.

The Industrial versus Restorative Age

The business world has changed considerably in the past century, progressing from the Industrial Age to what many are calling the Information Age. I prefer a different term for the current period—the Restorative Age—coined by Kim McManus, faculty director of George Washington University's Executive Leadership Education Program. In a moment I'll explain why. But for now let's examine the Industrial Age.

I talked with Ruth Holly, who worked as civilian payroll supervisor at the Pentagon in the late 1940s and early '50s, about the working environment at that time, its leadership style, and the effect on employees. She had some valuable observations.

"Sitting in a community lecture series," Ruth began, "I listened intently as a man elaborated on the development of the industrial system in the world. My mind slipped back to my first work situation. It, too, followed 'production line' methods and hierarchical leadership. I remember my dissatisfaction because I felt so unappreciated, as if my ideas were irrelevant—even silly—in the eyes of my supervisor. . . . I realize now that I wasn't prepared for the rigid management system employed at that time. Thinking my contribution would be valued and that, in the end, I'd be recognized as a valuable asset to the office where I worked, I soon learned that my contribution would never be noticed, and that any commendation—or increased salary—would belong to my immediate supervisor."

Obviously, there was something wrong with this system. But why did it develop in the first place? Ruth had some ideas about that.

"In industry, owners made a life-changing discovery: the production line. Facilitating increased productivity, it offered the most immediate solution to increasing demand. By assigning one task and only one task to each worker, the product could be developed systematically and completely. The problem with the method was that the worker and his contribution were generally ignored. His sense of worth was devalued. He became a robot.

"The fact that man doesn't want to be a simple cog in a huge wheel... was not taken into consideration. Worker dissatisfaction resulted and the rise of labor unions began. The labor unions addressed the dissatisfaction by saying in essence, 'Okay, your employer doesn't value your work or you as an individual. So we'll create a different value system. We'll make them pay. Money will be the reward for your hard work and dedication. We'll see that you get more money and more benefits. Then you'll feel compensated somewhat.' Money replaced praise. In fact money *became* praise.

"The more money a man earned, the better his self-image. In fact, his family and neighbors began to judge him by the amount of money he had to spend for luxuries, needs, and desires. Money became the driving force for society. But was it enough?"

Applying that thought to her own situation, Ruth realized that mere money wasn't enough for her. Oh, she got promotions and raises at her job, simply because she followed the rules. "Any creativity I brought to the job was ignored," she says. "Only my ability to perform as required resulted in recognition. No one in leadership really cared about me or my true worth."

Recently, however, Ruth worked in a team situation in which she was honored for her creativity. People encouraged her to think and evaluate, to try new things that might succeed or fail. "I felt released to do what God had willed for me," she says. "My mind was freed to consider performing not for money, but for the satisfaction of doing something that could be unique, something no one else had done."

Ruth's experience gave her new insight, which she brought to bear on the lecture praising the Industrial Revolution. "He skipped over the negative aspect—the disillusioned workers, the increased competitiveness and concentration on money as the only reward for success. I wanted to interrupt him, to challenge him, to remind him of the unmotivated workers, the loss of a quality product. Yet I remembered that more and more people are becoming aware that personal satisfaction is gained not only for a job well done but for recognition of personal contribution and creative efforts. These changes have resulted in happier employees, better work conditions, and an increased sense of personal self-worth by employees."

The hierarchical management style that has dominated the twentieth century workplace in America is quickly disappearing. In its place a more "restorative" style has developed, capitalizing on employee resources with decreased reliance on the previously exploited and controlled methods of supervision. Instead, employees are encouraged to develop their abilities and strengths to benefit the whole team.

In *Turbulent Mirror,* Briggs and Peat note the "ultimate irrelevance of hierarchy." Business leaders like to think that their chain of command gets things done right, but the hierarchy really doesn't matter much "when an airliner crashes because of a malfunctioning $2.00 bolt. The person who manufactured the bolt was at the bottom of the hierarchy of people who built the plane and yet was sufficient to topple the hierarchy."[3]

In an address to National Leaders Conference's Leadership Training Council, Kim McManus described the previous hierarchical leadership pattern: "As leaders, our first task is to put on hold all of our misconceptions or preconceptions or prior ideas—all the images and paradigms that we hold in our heads about what leadership is, what organizations look like, and what individuals in organizations are all about. And so begin to change our way of thinking to a more organismic or more interdependent way of thinking."[4]

In the same way that the environmental movement has forced us to turn away from exploiting nature and restore our natural resources, we are turning away from exploiting human resources in favor of developing and appreciating them. McManus continues, "In an industrial economy, we put a lot of emphasis on command and controls and a lot of emphasis on control of information, on linear chains of command. In an information age, what becomes most important are networks."[5]

Before we apply the Chaos Factor specifically, let's create a chart that shows the differences between a hierarchical leadership style and change-management thinking.

Hierarchical Leadership	Change Management
Result of Industrial Age based on linear, logical thinking	Result of Information Age based on a search for congruence (similarity) among multifaceted elements or ideas
Newtonian thinking claimed all decisions must be based on logical scientific thinking that retains a level of objectivity—management isolation and reticence with employees is a result	New scientific discovery in the physical and social sciences proves that there's no objectivity in science. We have some influence on everything we observe and touch—management participation with employees is a result.
Chaos demanding change is resisted and avoided	Chaos is anticipated and integrated

Organizational Format:

Main responsibility lies with upper management	Shared responsibility as workers are responsible for individual actions and contribute to the success of the larger whole
Production line mentality	Creative "clustering" mentality
Leadership leveled in pyramid structure	Leadership "clustered" in "networking" format

Methods:

Expects a controlled atmosphere with a rigid chain of command and organized linear systems of thought	Thrives in an open atmosphere in which interdependence of ideas and individuals is promoted
Upper level leadership uses lower level workers for personal gain	All employees equally respected for their character and valued for their contributions
Rigid rules demand obedience and compliance without question	Limited structuring is implemented to the degree it enhances participation and effectiveness

Hierarchical Leadership	Change Management
Creativity is stifled by enforced behavior patterns	Creativity is encouraged with a desire to incorporate new and innovative approaches
Status quo is demanded	Innovative thinking is rewarded
Cloning of workers sought	Uniqueness of individuals desired
Value, responsibility, and power controlled by leadership	Value, responsibility, and power invested in the individual
Change at the lower levels has little or no recognized effect on the larger organization	The smallest of changes precipitated by any individual in the complex system makes an impact on the larger organization
Dispassionate, objective forms of communication entailing much paperwork due to dependence on memorandums	Concerned communication with awareness of verbal and nonverbal communication skills and numerous one-on-one and group encounters
Works hard to control the effect of actions to dominate the environment and those in it	Expects the unexpected; free of the need to dominate but instead desires the mutual discovery of the good for the benefit of the whole
Looks for cause and effect	Sets up conditions that accept random input and direction while anticipating chaos giving new birth to order
Disillusioned frustration and later apathy result	Enthusiastic participation results

If change management is truly the wave of the future, how can you effectively prepare yourself for the work environment of the twenty-first century? Let me suggest that the Chaos Factor gives you a head start. You're already dealing with basic principles that will enable you to grow, rather than suffer, through the chaotic changes of your work situation. So let's see how the Chaos Factor and change management will specifically help you deal with the stress of the workplace.

Step 1: Acknowledge that chaos is the raw material of life. Abandoning the rigid systems of the past, employers are gradually bringing into the workplace an understanding of chaos, and they're capitalizing on this understanding as they prepare innovative products that keep them in step with the consumers and ahead of the competition. Joseph M. Arceri of the Praxis Consulting Group has written, "Another kind of contemporary change concerns fundamental shifts in our goals, structures, markets, and work environment. Often these changes pull the rug out from under us. These kinds of changes don't just add a new wrinkle to our everyday world; they radically call that world into question. It is this kind of change that we need to initiate if we are to respond appropriately to our continually evolving and changing business environment."[6]

Change in our culture is happening faster than we could have imagined, and it demands the acceptance of chaos. To stay abreast of the business world, managers and employees alike must begin to see change as an advantageous element—one that stimulates new ideas, creates desirable products, and opens our world to exciting possibilities.

Step 2: Recognize your responses of resistance to chaos and face the truth. Hierarchical thinking dies hard. Change management may be the wave of the future, but thousands of companies are still wading along in the past, conducting business as usual. New ideas are swept away with "We've never done it that way before." Chaos in the marketplace just drives these companies back to their obsolete systems. They'll pass the buck from department to department until there are no more bucks to pass.

Some of this is blindness—a refusal to see that the business world is changing, that this roller-coaster world *demands* change. Much of it is a slavish devotion to structuring. When a problem arises, draw a flow chart and organize your way out of it. As we've seen on the personal level, these resistance mechanisms just keep you from acknowledging the truth: that chaos exists and you need to roll with it.

Sadly, we see a sort of generation gap in business these days. Older managers and workers have functioned for decades in hierarchical systems. New methods can threaten them. Though there's no substitute for experience, younger people often bring better flexibility and creativity to the workplace, as well as more up-to-date education.

As a result, companies with an older hierarchy can lose younger employees who just don't fit the system. But when new executives take over, with their change-management methods, many older workers find it hard to adjust. There has to be a way to benefit from the strength of both young and old, blending innovation with experience. Each is valuable in the acceptance and integration of chaos.

Step 3: Abandon your faulty systems for chaos management. Success in the workplace requires that you put aside the past and focus on the present. What worked last year or last decade probably won't work today. And unfortunately for the older employee, a track record doesn't matter much anymore. What have you done for your company *lately?*

Therefore, older workers must be encouraged to accept new ways of thinking, overcoming their resistance to innovation and their idolatrous commitment to the hierarchical system. They need to de-emphasize the vertical structures while focusing more on horizontal structures, developing greater rapport with the other workers on the team.

How can you do this? Here are suggestions for employees of any age.

1. *Become a mentor.* Take time to get to know and appreciate your coworkers, perhaps inviting them to have lunch with you. Identify their strengths and help develop those strengths. Show appreciation for the contributions of oth-

ers. Help others when asked, but without a know-it-all attitude. And never be afraid to ask others for help.
2. *Project vitality.* If you're older, you don't need to dress like a teenager, but good health and fitness are attractive for any age. Stay current with trends in your field. Subscribe to the best trade periodical in your field to keep up with new ideas and technological advances. Brush up on computer skills, even taking a course if necessary.

To be competitive and remain secure in your position, you must continue to learn. The American Association of Retired Persons reports that "half of what you need to know today to do your job will probably be obsolete by the year 2000." To incorporate the theories of the Chaos Factor, give up faulty systems of chaos management and embrace progress and change. Take courses, attend seminars, be alert to new ideas and equipment used in the office.
3. *Meet with your boss and ask how you can make yourself more valuable to the organization.* Instead of being intimidated, learn to be a team player. Be careful not to be patronizing. Show you are willing to contribute to the success of your boss and the organization. Develop your area of expertise to the fullest, work independently and responsibly, but then present your findings and ideas to the team. Think of yourself as a member of a team on which your unique contribution is valued. Though theoretically no one is indispensable, if you are adept in your field and continue to grasp new challenges that broaden and enhance your capabilities, you will offer something that no one else can—your unique skills, abilities, and experience.
4. *Keep accurate records of your work and the comments it solicits.* To build your own confidence and sense of accomplishment as well as to demonstrate your contribution to the corporation, it's always wise to record your participation. It simply helps you monitor your effectiveness and may aid you in identifying weak areas that need strengthening. It's much more effective if you sign up for a new

class, develop a new skill advantageous to your job, or create new opportunities for growth without previous suggestion from your coworkers.[7]

Choosing to embrace this approach to chaos in the workplace will relieve the stress we discussed at the opening of this chapter. *Step 4: Discover peace in life's process.* Appreciating the process is a key element of change management. We see the process most clearly in two trends, networking and clustering.

Networking is simply a loose organization of individuals who meet for the purpose of communication. Perhaps the most basic form these days is the Internet. There anyone can connect with anyone else to transfer ideas and information. Each individual has equal access to information. Equal respect is given to each person's opinions.

Change management employs networking by placing employees in small groups without hierarchies. Each employee possesses an area of expertise and that knowledge contributes significantly to the whole. Whether considering an immediate problem or long-term goals, members of the network gather to "cluster" ideas. These ideas are then evaluated, developed, and acted on, based on group consensus or the consensus of the leadership team.

Networking creates new horizontal connections as opposed to the vertical chain-of-command system of the past. In theory, it can provide a safe environment for ideas to be pooled and developed. It also fosters communication among various parts of a company, while hierarchical systems tend to isolate departments. Economist Robert Theobald, founder of a network for social entrepreneurs, writes, "Linkage and networks are going to be the primary and recognized way to get things done in the future."[8]

Of course, networking occurs in various ways, official and unofficial. You can network with your neighbor over the back fence or a friend in the church lobby. In every case, though, it's an expansion of your own resources by interacting with the resources of someone else, often someone with a completely different specialty.

Interestingly, women seem to be naturally better at networking than men. Dr. James Campbell Quick, editor of *The Journal of Occupational Health Psychology,* writes, "Women are better at establishing friendships and networking, so if something goes wrong in their professional or personal lives, they have several women from whom they can get emotional support and help. Women help each other in the office, unlike many men. The female executives we surveyed reported that they got support and honest feedback from the women who worked for them, and they responded by helping female employees develop their skills so they would advance in their careers."

An added benefit: Female executives respond better to stress than their male counterparts, even with their added home and child-care responsibilities.[9]

Clustering is a technique used (often within networking situations) to stimulate creativity. Essentially, it's what we used to call brainstorming, but with even less pressure to reach a solution. Whether or not your workplace employs it, you can use this method to enhance your thinking.

In a way, clustering accepts and embraces the chaos in our minds. Rather than rigidly excluding any thoughts that don't offer an immediate solution to the problem at hand, we allow thinking to flow freely. We entertain ideas that may not have any immediate payoff, because we recognize that chaos can help us in surprising ways.

Writing instructors use clustering to spark ideas in their students. A teacher might write a word on a chalkboard and ask the students to come up with related words, whatever comes to mind. Then, with a cluster of words in front of them, the students might be inspired to write a story or article.

But the same method can be used in a business environment, as workers cluster ideas around a product, service, marketing theme, or consumer need. The important thing is to let the chaotic process flow, developing any idea, no matter how wacky it seems.

"As you cluster, you may experience a sense of randomness, an uneasy sense that it isn't leading anywhere," says Gabriele

Rico in *Writing the Natural Way.* "That is your logical mind wanting to get into the act and let you know how foolish you are. Clustering not only unblocks and releases, it also generates inspiration and insight. The receptive mind is programmed with novelty, ambiguity, and the unknown. Ideas come of their own accord."[10]

Clustering not only anticipates chaos but depends on it to give birth to new ideas and thoughts. You can see how it might be threatening to those who are committed to hierarchical systems, but innovative companies are using methods like this to break new ground.

Rather than applying linear thinking, clustering equips the participant to recognize congruent ideas—ideas that agree, correspond, and are harmonious. Discovering and developing the congruent element brings innovation.

In his new book, *Thriving on Chaos,* management consultant Tom Peters advises managers that "in today's volatile world markets the only way to flourish is to 'love chaos' by creating a highly nonlinear environment without the company, involving everyone in everything in order to foster creative breakthroughs."[11]

Step 5: Let go of your control. Contemporary business is an increasingly fluid and uncertain environment. Within this environment, chaos can flourish and give birth to order. Learning to give up control by anticipating new and unexpected changes frees each member of the organization to implement change. It's risky, of course. There are no sure bets. But in today's volatile world, those who play it safe are likely to be left in the dust.

In *Harvard Business Review,* Robert Katz notes, "Management necessarily involves always thinking in terms of the following: relative emphasis and priorities among conflicting objectives and criteria; relative tendencies and probabilities (rather than certainties); rough correlations and patterns among elements (rather than clear-cut cause and effect relationships)."[12]

Do you see all the uncertainties in that statement? Nowadays the good manager isn't the one who develops that one and only method that will absolutely, positively work. No, he or she needs to weigh priorities and judge the probabilities, gauging the tendencies and perceiving "rough correlations." It's not an exact science. Chaos is always around you. The good manager is the one who learns to play with it.

Step 6: Evaluate the options, make choices, and integrate the chaos. How can you effectively evaluate the options, make choices consistent with the Chaos Factor, and integrate the chaos? I've gathered various tips from people who are working effectively in this change-sensitive environment.

1. Educate yourself concerning contemporary society and the radical changes taking place every day in business, technology, and society.
2. Develop your unique skills and abilities to become a creative, supportive team player in your situation.
3. Develop better communication skills so that your verbal and nonverbal communications are sensitive and interactive, demonstrating a relationship as well as task orientation. Both must be kept in balance.
4. Cooperate with others and develop the team mind-set that's necessary in today's workplace. Look upon other employees as gifted, talented contributors to be respected and appreciated rather than as competitors to be controlled.
5. Develop your sense of purpose so that you bring confidence and responsibility to your area of expertise.
6. Plan, diagnose, and anticipate change, searching for congruence in multifaceted thoughts. This gives birth to new ideas and innovations.
7. Be creative and flexible, so you're prepared to move with new direction or development.
8. Always consider the big-picture view while perfecting your contribution. This may lead to new discoveries in your field as you seek to enhance the organization.
9. If you're a manager, search for new ways to integrate employees into the change process. They need to "own" the process and feel their contributions are not only significant but essential to the success of the whole.

10. Get set to cope with the unpredictable. Rather than dread chaos and change, look on it as a challenge to be enjoyed, a problem to be overcome.
11. Commend your coworkers for their contributions. Build a sense of respect for each individual.

Dr. Salvatore R. Maddi, professor of psychology at the University of California at Irvine and president of the Hardiness Institute at Irvine, studied executives at Illinois Bell to see how they coped with the breakup of their company. The ones who thrived, Maddi observes, "viewed the changes as challenges rather than threats, then found something they could control, like coming up with a new product."[13]

Stress Busters

We began this chapter by acknowledging the stress that results from resisting chaos in the workplace. Here are some final stress busters drawn from the suggestions of management psychologist Dr. John H. Howard.[14]

Stress Buster 1. Don't procrastinate and spend the majority of your time on low-priority projects. When you neglect the higher-priority responsibilities, a crisis is inevitable. Develop specific goals and conform the time allotments of your day to these goals, designating the majority of your time to the accomplishment of the most important goals.

Stress Buster 2. Give up your need to control things that are completely out of your reach. Let go. Uncooperative coworkers rarely change. Take responsibility for your own actions and your actions alone. A great deal of energy can be lost trying to fix a situation or relationship that is not really your problem. Develop an objectivity that enables you to say, "That's their problem, not mine." Hope the best for them, and then go on to fulfill your own responsibilities to the best of your ability.

Stress Buster 3. Don't work over your lunch hour by inviting a business partner to lunch to discuss some aspect of the job. See your lunch as a psychological break. You need it to work most effectively for the remainder of the day.

Stress Buster 4. Are you a chronic "hurrier," always rushing, always on an overcommitted schedule? "Cultivate good judgment and decision, not speed," writes Howard.

Stress Buster 5. If you're working fifty- and sixty-hour weeks, cut back. Productivity decreases in highly stressed, overworked people.

Stress Buster 6. If a stressful activity is ahead, imagine yourself walking through the experience. Anticipate known and unknown problems, then consider each detail so that you can enter the situation with confidence.

Stress Buster 7. When you feel tense, take a moment to relax your aching muscles. Take a deep breath. Relax each part of your body before returning to the task.

Stress Buster 8. Listen to music at least ten minutes each day. Music breaks go far in reducing stress and anxiety.

Stress Buster 9. Learn to confide in a variety of individuals on different subjects at different times so as to create a support group. Offer the same benefit to those around you. Knowing someone else is praying for you may be the greatest support you'll find.

Stress Buster 10. Laugh. Whether buying books of *Far Side* cartoons, watching movie comedies, or getting together with friends who make you laugh, arrange situations that help you laugh every day.

Finding Rest in the Midst of Chaos

As for me, the effect of this has been to teach me to rest more utterly than ever in the sweet will of God.

Hannah W. Smith

The brisk clip of my stride slowed as I passed something extraordinary.

On my daily walk I spend time thinking, enjoying creation's beauty, wondering what goes on in the lives of those behind closed doors. I reflect on the world, life, and my part in it. My walk takes me through an apartment complex. The layout of the complex is designed to provide the privacy and atmosphere of a home in the woods. Maples and oaks shade each section. Squirrels scamper from tree to tree while songbirds delight their listeners. Yet the grounds definitely display the handiwork of professional gardeners and groundskeepers. The standard azaleas, expected chrysanthemums, and flowing pompous grass are uniformly spaced with precision. Since I walk this path daily, I usually take little notice of these surroundings.

But something was different. Passing by one section of the complex, I paused and then stopped to admire an unexpected sight. There, clustered around a corner of the building, was an English garden. It appeared out of place. Scattered among red roses and white geraniums were the tall spikes of lavender delphiniums, entwined with tumbled yellow, pink, and purple wildflowers.

Nestled close to the garden were a green-painted park bench, a round metal table, and two chairs. In the midst of this sterile, professionally maintained complex, someone had created a personal "secret garden," a refuge from the rush and race of our world.

It seemed to represent a place of rest, a haven in the midst of the chaos of life. I was fascinated. Who was its owner? What caused her or him to create such beauty in this small corner of the world? I was soon to find my answers. Two days later on my midday walk, I couldn't wait to reach the garden in the hope that its mysterious owner would be present. I was not disappointed. There she sat, chatting with neighbors. Blond hair, suntanned face, blue eyes, and the crinkled smile of age. Merriment animated her conversation and communicated warmth and interest. Though I wanted to stop and ask her the questions that intrigued me, I didn't want to disturb her. I continued on.

Yesterday, my opportunity came. When I passed, she and a different set of friends rested under the shade of an oak, sipping lemonade. Again I hesitated, but after circling the block a little later, I saw my opportunity. The friends were gone. I gathered my courage and stopped to talk.

"Hello. I wanted to tell you how much I've admired your garden," I said with a smile. "It's lovely. It reminds me of English gardens I saw in London several years ago."

"Yes!" she exclaimed, obviously pleased I recognized her intent. "I love it, too. It helps me make friends. Other people enjoy it so much. They come to meet me, just like you."

"Have you had beautiful gardens all your life and now you've created this one here as well?" I questioned.

She paused to consider. "Well, in a way, I guess. My husband's company constantly transferred us. We moved thirty times in forty years. My husband would choose any old place for us to live. He would go ahead to each town and find a house. I would follow and then do whatever it took to fix it up. I've planted flowers, trees, you can't even imagine all the things I've done to make our houses feel like home.

"My husband passed on. So now this is home. I love my flowers and herbs. Others come to talk to me just as you've done, and I make friends. Some people just come alone and sit here even when I'm not home. They seem to find rest here."

Discovering Rest

"They seem to find rest here." As I introduce the final step in the Chaos Factor, I consider the words of this new friend, Beverly Potter. Rest is something we all desperately want, yet it always seems to elude us. Somehow, in our own ways and times, we all need to find a secret garden of our own, a place of rest and beauty. Step 7 is to find rest as chaos gives birth to order.

I read the poem of an unknown author recently that challenged me to reconsider the pursuits of my life.

> First I was dying to finish high school and start college.
> And then I was dying to finish college and start working.
> And then I was dying to marry and have children.
> And then I was dying for my children to grow old enough for
>   school so I could return to work.
> And then I was dying to retire.
> And now, I am dying . . . and suddenly I realize I
>   forgot to live.

It's the way of our world, isn't it? We're so busy trying to get through today and grab hold of the future that we forget to live today. Plagued by busyness, dominated by hectic schedules, and intent on conquering the chaos, we never experience rest.

Yet rest is imperative for health and sanity. Rest refreshes the soul and gives meaning and purpose to the pursuit. Rest is a gift. Rest is the final reward of the Chaos Factor. When we follow the steps and apply them to every aspect of life, we can rest. By discovering peace in the process, security in one greater than ourselves, and trust in his orchestration of the chaos, our souls rest. It's actually the experience, example, and promise of the God of the universe.

Our Promised Rest

We read in the biblical account of creation, "By the seventh day God had finished the work he had been doing; so on the seventh day he rested from all his work. And God blessed the seventh day and made it holy, because on it he rested from all the work of creating that he had done."[1] The God who designed order from the chaos and created form from that primordial void, rested. And he promises a rest for us as well. The author of the Book of Hebrews says of it, "There remains, then, a Sabbath-rest for the people of God; for anyone who enters God's rest also rests from his own work, just as God did from his. Let us, therefore, make every effort to enter that rest."[2]

Step 7: Find rest as chaos gives birth to order.

Rest. I sought it for years. But I never understood it until several months ago. Rest is the end of the struggle with chaos. Let me explain.

As I began my journey into chaos, identifying my own chaos resistance systems, abandoning faulty coping mechanisms, and particularly giving up the need to control my world and those in it, I began to experience a new freedom. I had been buried in busyness, always feeling that I was racing somewhere . . . but where? I was never quite sure. I have no idea why so many things became so important, why they became the driving force of my life. All I know is that I was a long way down this road of stress and distraction before I realized it—and then I didn't know how to get back. Finally, through the understanding of the Chaos Factor and the process of reevaluation and change, I began the journey back toward peace, forward toward rest.

One thing I hadn't expected but soon discovered was that the Chaos Factor carried wonderful benefits. Maybe you have already begun to experience some of these.

Unexpected Freedom

Relinquishing control and accepting chaos gave way to freedom. I remember the first time I came across this statement and realized what I had been doing to myself for many years. It read:

> Do what you've never done before
> See what you've never seen
> Feel what you've never felt before,
> Say what you've never said,
> Bear what you've never borne before
> Hear what you've never heard.
> All is not what it would seem;
> Nothing ever remains the same.
> Change is life's characteristic;
> Bend and flow and play the game . . .
> *So many times I was the one*
> *Who stopped myself from doing things;*
> *So many times I was the one*
> *Who grounded myself and clipped my wings.*
>
> emphasis added

And so often I had. How many times had I clipped my wings without even realizing it? Life became a misery to endure rather than a mystery to uncover. Now I make it a point to experience new things. A phrase I had considered so saccharine began to make sense: "Stop and smell the roses." I decided to take time to enjoy life. I spent more time with my children, enjoying the simple pleasures of their laughter and companionship.

I stopped pushing myself so hard, trusting the Divine Conductor to orchestrate the harmonies of my life better than I could. I chose to enjoy life in the process, acknowledging his control and relinquishing mine. Life became fun, with new surprises around every corner.

What are you killing yourself to accomplish, anyway? I would ask myself. *What is it all worth in light of eternity? Will the things that seem so important today, even life-threatening, really have an enduring significance in the long run of life? When I look back on my life, will I have memories worth cherishing or only regrets?*

These questions began to order my life, changing my priorities and pursuits. Just as I stopped beside Beverly Potter's secret garden to talk with her and learn more about her as an individual who mattered in this huge scheme of life, I talked with others. I began to choose relationships over tasks and people over pressure. I felt I had been granted a new opportunity for life.

Recaptured Joy

And what did I discover in the process? Joy.

This wasn't totally new to me. As a teenager, I was known for my joyous demeanor. Life for me was a present to open, a gift to be appreciated. I found great joy in my relationship with this God of the universe who became my Father when faith in his Son, Jesus Christ, poured excitement and abundance into my life.

But somewhere amid the demands, pressures, unrealistic expectations, and disappointments, I lost joy. I didn't know how to recapture it until the Chaos Factor entered my life. Then I began to understand it. When I had tried to organize chaos out of my life, I had lost peace, hope, and joy. Just as a child loses innocence, I had lost my sense of the meaning of this earthly existence.

Then one day I realized that, without my noticing, joy had spontaneously returned. With the Chaos Factor and the freedom it supplied, I had time to laugh. Time to play. Time to rejoice.

I began to understand that joy was something God not only had created but *experienced*. People rarely think of God as joyful. What a shame! It's one of his most important qualities, and something he longs to share with us. When Jesus spoke to his Father in preparation for his ascension from this earth, he said, "I am coming to you now, but I say these things while I am still in the world, so that they may have the full measure of my joy within them."[3] Can you imagine what the full measure of the God of the universe must be? I can't. But it must be a lot of joy—and he offers it to us as a gift.

Then I found this simple definition for joy.

Some Signs and Symptoms of Inner Joy

A tendency to think and act spontaneously rather than on fears based on experience.

An unmistakable ability to enjoy each moment.

A loss of interest in judging other people.

A loss of interest in interpreting the actions of others.

A loss of interest in conflict.

A loss of the ability to worry. (This is a very serious symptom.)

Frequent overwhelming episodes of appreciation.

Contented feeling of connectedness with others and with creation.

Frequent attacks of outrageous laughter.

An increased tendency to let things happen rather than to make them happen.

An increased susceptibility to the love extended by others as well as an uncontrollable urge to extend it.

Warning: If you have some or all of the above symptoms, please be advised that your condition of inner joy may be so far advanced as not to be curable. If you are exposed to anyone exhibiting any of these symptoms, remain exposed only at your own risk.

Unconditional Love Gave Way to Unconditional Acceptance

I stopped trying so hard to be perfect and instead chose to accept love from God and others. As I relinquished control, I came to realize there was a tyrannical dictator in my life who needed to be dethroned: me. When I accepted the Creator God's unconditional love for me by yielding to the love of his Son, I realized that his love was a free gift, one I could do nothing to earn. Yet as time passed, I reverted to the old desires to earn his affection, just as I had desperately tried to earn my earthly father's love. In spite of my father's rage, I spent a lifetime trying to please him, and I slipped into the same ways with God.

I tried very hard to be perfect for him. Attempting the impossible demanded more and more control. The more I tried to control life, the harder I became. My inner voice became the barking sergeant that enlisted men despise. But I didn't bark at others, only myself. I quickly criticized my every fault and despised my every weakness.

As I began to embrace the Chaos Factor, I continued to learn to accept my imperfections and weaknesses. God loves me anyway. When I find myself choosing to ignore God's instructions, I experience sincere regret, change directions, and return to his way. In a new way, I appreciate the fact that God loves and uses imperfect people every day.

I find it interesting that the admired apostles of the Bible were human just like us. They had their own weaknesses and shortcomings. I found this amusing "memo" that points this out:

MEMO

To: Jesus, Son of Joseph
From: Jordan Management Consultants

Thank you for submitting the resumes of the 12 men you have picked for management positions in your new organization. All of them have now taken our battery of tests, and we have not only run the results through our computer, but also arranged personal interviews for each of them with our psychologist and vocational aptitude consultant.

The profiles of all tests are included, and you will want to study them carefully. As part of our service we will make some general comments. These are given as a result of staff consultations and come without any additional fee.

It is the staff opinion that most of your nominees are lacking in background, education, and vocational aptitude for the type of enterprise you are undertaking. They do not have the team concept. We recommend that you continue your search.

Simon Peter is emotionally unstable and given to fits of temper. Andrew has absolutely no qualities of leadership. The brothers, James and John, place personal interest above company loyalty. Thomas has a skeptical attitude that would tend to undermine morale. It is our duty to tell you that Matthew has been blacklisted by the Greater Jerusalem Better Business Bureau. James, the son of Alphaeus, and Thaddeus have radical leanings and show a high score on the manic-depressive scale.

Only one shows great potential—ability, resourcefulness, a business mind, meets people well, ambitious, highly motivated. We recommend Judas Iscariot as your controller and right-hand man.[4]

God works with imperfect people! As I grew to understand this, my attitudes changed. I began to dispose of exaggerated expectations for myself and to loosen the grip of my perfectionistic tendencies. I was learning to accept myself as I was. Gradual and permanent changes continued.

I became more relaxed, realizing that I was valuable to God and he would work with me in strengthening weaknesses and removing flaws. His love proved deeper than my deepest trespass.

There's a story about a young man who came to Mother Teresa for advice. In anticipation of this much-awaited event, he had considered all the situations and problems he wanted to describe in detail, hoping for her insights.

Finally the day arrived. He met with her alone and spent ten minutes pouring out his heart's concerns. When he finished, Mother Teresa was silent. Then she said one thing: "Well, when you spend one hour a day adoring your Lord and never do anything which you know is wrong . . . you will be fine!" Shocked by the simple truth of her reply, he excused himself so others could greet her.

She was right. Often we make life too difficult for ourselves. If we simply appreciated the Chaos Factor, trusted God, and relaxed in his life process, we would know the relief and peace we so greatly need. It reminds me of a hymn sung regularly in the church I attended as a child, "Trust and obey, for there's no other way to be happy in Jesus, but to trust and obey." I always saw obedience as an arduous task, rarely accomplished. I now see it as the natural response of a love relationship with God. Adore God, do what you know is right according to God's book, the Bible, and with his assistance, all else will find resolve in the ebb and flow of life's process.

Entering into Rest

These positive, exciting benefits continued to fill my life. Then nine months ago, the bottom dropped out again.

It was August. Summer always proved difficult financially for my nonprofit organization, but this summer practically destroyed it. I'd contacted everyone I knew who might be interested in helping, but with little response. Our choices were all dismal: keep the company going (sinking more deeply into debt) or go bankrupt (not ethically acceptable to us). I felt trapped.

At the same time, my husband's recent career change left insufficient funds to pay family expenses. To save costs, we decided to move out of town to a small cottage we owned. My husband secured a part-time position, but we were still short of money.

Now our family faced chaos on multiple fronts, adjusting to a new home in a town two hours away, a new job, less money, and a questionable future. My anxiety rose with each day. I desperately needed direction, yet no one seemed to have answers.

How did I respond to this tailspin? I must say I expected myself to sink into feelings of devastation, as I had done in previous crises. But I applied the Chaos Factor, following the steps outlined in this book. Rather than being shocked, surprised, and overwhelmed by the crisis, I accepted it as a normal part of life. Rather than turning to my familiar resistance systems for protection and security, I chose to trust the Divine Orchestrator to continue his work. I accepted the process.

Instead of trying to control my situation by creating alternatives, forcing issues, or demanding that others solve the problems, I let go and waited for God's plan to unfold in his time. This crisis became my lab experience for the Chaos Factor. Finally enough incidents were converging at once to test everything I had learned over the previous seven years. Would it work? Could I apply the principles and follow the steps even when I felt that everything was unraveling?

Supernatural Intervention

As I sought God's direction in the Bible, I came across an interesting story about three friends of Jesus: Lazarus and his sisters Martha and Mary.[5]

Lazarus was dying. His sisters sent word to Jesus, assuming he would come as quickly as possible to heal him, as they had seen him heal so many others before. But Jesus waited two days before setting out for their town. By the time Jesus arrived, Lazarus was dead and buried.

Neither Martha nor Mary could understand why Jesus hadn't been there. Didn't he love them? How could he simply not show up? Each complained, "Lord, if you had been here, my brother would not have died."

As I read their story, I realized I felt very much as they did. *God, I'm trusting you, but what are you doing? I don't get it. None of this makes sense.*

But I discovered that the Lord had something very different in mind than Martha and Mary imagined—something better than their expectations. He wanted them to come to know him in a new way, and he chose the only method he knew would accomplish that purpose.

They already understood certain things about him. Martha stated what she knew, "Even now God will give you whatever you ask."

Jesus replied, "Your brother will rise again."

Martha countered, "I know he will rise again in the resurrection at the last day."

But Jesus had a different perspective. He answered, "I *am* the resurrection and the life. He who believes in me will live, even though he dies; and whoever lives and believes in me will never die. Do you believe this?"

In other words, don't give me some intellectual jargon about "someday." I'm talking about now. Right this minute. I *am* the resurrection. It's not something I will simply do at some time or another. It is who I *am*. I can raise Lazarus this minute if I choose. I *am* life itself.

Again Martha parroted what she had learned. "Yes, Lord. I believe that you are the Christ, the Son of God, who was to come into the world." Martha's words were genuine but inadequate. She believed what she said about Jesus, the future, and the past. But what about the present? Was Jesus insufficient for the present situation? Was his power diminished?

At this point Jesus, deeply troubled, went to the tomb. "Take away the stone," he ordered. Martha's next words show the limitations of her faith. "But, Lord, by this time there is a bad odor, for he has been there four days."

Jesus patiently responded, "Did I not tell you that if you believed, you would see the glory of God?"

Such a simple statement. Yet as I read it, I knew the question applied to me as well. I was much like Martha. I knew the right things to believe. I believed they were true, but I missed the power behind the truth. God was and is big enough for me to trust. He knows exactly what he is doing even when I don't (which is most of the time). I'm finite; he's infinite. Even when I don't understand, even when I've followed the Chaos Factor and trusted the God of chaos, even when I try to figure out the situation and his role in it—*if I would simply believe,* I would see the glory of God.

Seeing the glory of God is a life-changing thing. "Glory" in the Bible means the unveiled beauty and magnificence of God. It means those attributes beyond our comprehension that God possesses, demonstrated on the stage of our earthly existence. It means that God makes an appearance in your everyday life. It means his miracles and mysteries become part of you. God wants to show you new aspects of himself.

At Lazarus's graveside, Jesus prayed, "Father, I thank you that you have heard me. I know that you always hear me, but I said this for the benefit of the people standing here, that they may believe that you sent me."

Why didn't Jesus come when Martha and Mary called? Why did he delay his trip until Lazarus died? Why did he ask them to stop trying to make sense of it all and simply believe? Because he wanted them to meet God in their midst in a way they never had dreamed possible. He did it all for their benefit. God had a better idea.

What happened as a result? Not only was Lazarus raised, which was the thing of greatest concern to them, but they met the living God and saw his power—the glory of the God of the universe.

Jesus called out in a loud voice, "Lazarus, come out!" The dead man emerged with burial linen still wrapped around his hands, feet, and face. "Take off the grave clothes and let him go."

As I think about this story over and again, I am stopped by Jesus' question: Didn't I tell you that if you believe, you will see the glory of God?

I can't even imagine how many times God allows the chaos of our lives to baffle us so we will be willing simply to look at him and meet him in the supernatural way. He asks a simple question that contains the promise of a lifetime. "Didn't I already tell you that if you will merely believe . . . ?" Stop trying to figure it all out and make sense of it all. Stop trying to control everything

Embracing the Chaos

and fix what can't be fixed. Give up all your attempts to understand . . . and simply believe.

After being confronted with Martha's example, so much like my own, I decided to do exactly what Jesus desired. I decided to stop trying to figure out, understand, fix, or change my situation in the midst of crisis. I decided simply to believe. And an amazing thing happened: I experienced the most wonderful reward of God that could be discovered. I experienced rest. And it has been an abiding rest. Every time I feel anxious or my mind starts its struggles again, I choose to believe instead. And at the end of the struggle, I find rest.

When we discussed four of the six stages of change—precontemplation, contemplation, preparation, and action—I promised we would close with the final two. The fifth is maintenance. Simply put, maintenance is continuing in the steps begun. You now know every element of the Chaos Factor and can continue in it every day for the rest of your life. Some researchers question whether the final stage, termination, even exists. In the case of the Chaos Factor, the only termination comes when life on earth is no more, so this stage is not worth our consideration.

My situation improves daily, but that's not the most important thing. The glory is in my growing understanding of a God in whom I can rest, undisturbed by life's chaos and uncertainty.

The Bible describes this new experience I have enjoyed for months: "Let the beloved of the LORD rest secure in him, for he shields him all day long, and the one the LORD loves rests between his shoulders."[6] The picture is of a lamb resting on the back of its shepherd—safe, secure, and at peace.

And maybe the greatest secret held within Beverly's secret garden is this: With rest comes beauty. Rest produces beauty of soul, a beauty all can see. And that beauty invites others to come in and talk, to greet the God of chaos.

I hope the Chaos Factor offers you hope and a new perspective on life. I would love to hear the story of your journey through chaos.

In memory of Susan C. McKinney,
whose life and death enriched the lives of countless others,
and dedicated to the God in whom she put her trust.

The Chaos Factor

*Seven Life-Changing Steps
for Coping with Chaos*

Step 1: Acknowledge that chaos is the raw material of life.
Step 2: Recognize your responses of resistance to chaos and face the truth.
Step 3: Abandon your faulty systems for chaos management.
Step 4: Discover peace in life's process.
Step 5: Let go of your control.
Step 6: Evaluate the options, make choices, and integrate the chaos.
Step 7: Find rest as chaos gives birth to order.

Questions for Reflection

The Chaos Factor and You

If you have found *Dancing in the Storm* helpful and would enjoy considering the ideas and concepts of the Chaos Factor more thoroughly, gathering a small group of interested friends or acquaintances is a great way to start. The following are questions to trigger thoughts and discussions. Enjoy the journey!

Chapter 1

1. List five unforeseen interruptions that occurred in your day today. Note and describe each instance of chaos and the results.

2. List three chaotic events of the past (example: marriage, birth, death, unexpected move).

Event	Cause: Positive or Negative	Effect on You, Others
1.		
2.		
3.		

Questions for Reflection

How did these events significantly alter your lifestyle? What method did you use to deal with them?

Chapter 2

1. Look again at the symptoms of resistance listed in this chapter (for example, anger, complaining, blaming, deceit). What symptoms do you recognize in your life that point to personal chaos resistance?
2. Describe one incident in your life that demonstrates this symptom.
3. How do you cope with chaos when this symptom surfaces?

Chapter 3

1. Refer to the questionnaire, Methods for Chaos Management on pages 39–41. List the coping methods referred to in each question that reflect your structure system for responding to chaos.
2. List four chaotic incidents in which you used structure to manage chaos. Explain why structure as a coping mechanism was inevitably ineffective. Explain what caused you to employ this system.

Incident	Structuring Method	Ineffectiveness System Cause
1.		
2.		
3.		
4.		

3. Describe more fully your personal structuring system when you respond to chaos. What coping mechanisms do you employ?

Chapter 4

1. List all the coping mechanisms of the blindness system that you can think of. That is, how does a person choose blindness? What forms does it take? (You might want to refer to the test in chapter 2. See questions 6, 9, 12, 13, 14, 15, 16, 17, 18, 22.)

Then, at the right, put your thoughts about why these methods prove ineffective in dealing with chaos.

Questions for Reflection

Mechanism	Reason for Ultimate Ineffectiveness
1.	
2.	
3.	
4.	

2. Describe four incidents in your life when you employed the blindness technique to respond to chaos.

3. Describe your personal blindness methods for chaos management and the ineffectiveness of the results.

4. Which of the coping mechanisms in your structure or blindness systems for dealing with chaos are most difficult to consider abandoning? Which would you call personal idols and why?

5. How will you begin the process of abandoning these for a greater dependence on God?

Chapter 5

1. Describe any feelings of disillusionment you may have identified while reading this book. Have you allowed yourself to mourn? Take time to recognize that giving up unrealistic expectations frees you to experience and appreciate the richness of life as it is.

2. Consider the coping mechanisms and self-constructed idols you believe in and run to when confronted with chaos. Choose to abandon these for a God who will replace your idols with true security and peace.

3. Of the three types of pain described—disillusionment, loss, and repentance—which is the greatest pain for you? How does God comfort you in your mourning?

Chapter 6

1. Write one idea about the process of life in this chapter that seemed to apply best in your life.

2. Can you give one example of a "Plan B" choice you made? What were the consequences?

3. List two choices you made that changed the course of your life. Describe how these have blended into the fabric of your life.

Questions for Reflection

Chapter 7

1. List character qualities of control introduced in this chapter. Can you add others you've observed in yourself and others?

2. Describe one incident in which you worked to control others in the midst of a chaotic situation. What were the consequences of your controlling attitudes and actions? What were the reactions of those you wished to control?

3. How would you handle this situation differently if it happened again?

4. What new choices have you made concerning your future responses to chaos? List these choices and share them with a trusted friend who can encourage you in your endeavor to maintain new choices and replace ineffective systems of the past.

Chapter 8

1. Choose one day in your life and list your plans for that day in one column. Then, as the day goes on, list in another column the chaotic interruptions that occur.

2. Now copy the list of chaotic interruptions and describe how you responded to each one. Then evaluate your responses. Are you pleased with the way you handled the interruption? Or is there room for improvement?

Chaotic Interruption	Response	Evaluation
1.		
2.		
3.		
4.		

3. List three things you'd like to change about your responses to daily chaotic inconveniences. Suggest alternative behavior and create a strategy to accomplish it.

Chapter 9

1. Describe a traumatic crisis that has taken place in your life.

Questions for Reflection

2. How did you respond?
3. How would you like to respond differently in the future?
4. How has this crisis blended into the fabric of your life?
5. List benefits you or others gained as a result of this chaotic intervention.
6. If you are in a crisis, what aspects of the Chaos Factor can you apply today?

Chapter 10

1. Does your workplace have hierarchical leadership or a change-management style?
2. If it's hierarchical, what can you learn from the Chaos Factor that can benefit you and your coworkers in your situation?
3. If it's change management, what steps would you like to take to become an even stronger team member in your work environment?
4. How does stress affect you? How can your knowledge of the Chaos Factor help relieve your stress this week?

Chapter 11

1. Explain the seven steps of the Chaos Factor in your own words.
2. What valuable insight would you like to remember and implement as you confront chaos daily in the future?
3. List the six stages of change and identify where you are in this process. What would you need to reach an effective level of maintenance? How can these needs be met to facilitate new growth?
4. Describe your life journey with chaos in light of the Chaos Factor. Where are you, and where would you like to be?
5. What element of the Chaos Factor can you share with a friend who also struggles, and how can you encourage each other?
6. Share the Chaos Factor with three friends in the next week. The more you share it, the more beneficial it will be in your life.

Notes

Chapter 1: *Chaos*
1. James 1:17.
2. Gen. 1:1–2.
3. John Briggs and F. David Peat, *Turbulent Mirror: An Illustrated Guide to Chaos Theory and the Science of Wholeness* (New York: Harper and Row, 1989), 14, 20.
4. Tim McCarthy, "The Future Is Now: From Chaos to Cosmos," *National Catholic Reporter* (16 April 1993): 5.
5. Ibid., emphasis added.
6. Ibid.
7. Rom. 8:28 NASB.

Chapter 2: *Playing the Games of Resistance*
1. John Briggs and F. David Peat, *Turbulent Mirror: An Illustrated Guide to Chaos Theory and the Science of Wholeness* (New York: Harper and Row, 1989), 37.
2. Clifton Fadimon, ed., *The Little, Brown Book of Anecdotes* (Boston: Little, Brown, 1985), no. 28.
3. Exod. 15:23–24; 16:2.
4. Num. 14:26–28.
5. Gen. 19:14–26.
6. Eadimon, *Little, Brown Book of Anecdotes*, no. 1.
7. Gen. 3:12–13.
8. Mark 14:43–51.
9. Charles R. Swindoll, *Intimacy with the Almighty* (Dallas: Word, 1996), 9–10.
10. Gen. 16:1–4.
11. Job 6–7.

Chapter 3: *Structuring*

1. Mark 9.
2. Max Lucado, *He Still Moves Stones* (Dallas: Word, 1993), 128.
3. Matt. 5:48.
4. Ruth Senter, *Surrounded by Mystery* (Grand Rapids: Zondervan, 1988), 14.
5. Thomas Merton, *Thoughts in Solitude* (New York: Farrar, Straus, and Giovani, 1976), 83, adapted.

Chapter 4: *Going Blind*

1. Gen. 3:8–10.
2. Gen. 2:16–17.
3. Don Allender, "Marriage and Family" (CSL603, course for graduate studies at Colorado Christian University, conducted at the Foothills Campus, Morrison, Colorado).
4. Prov. 1:7.
5. Phil. 4:8.
6. Rom. 8:24.
7. Ps. 62:5.
8. Ps. 33:18.
9. Ps. 25:3, emphasis added.
10. Rom. 12:12.
11. Rom. 15:13.
12. Heb. 11:1.
13. Ps. 42:3.
14. Alice Kosner, "Making the Best of Change," *Cosmopolitan*, February 1992, 68.
15. Ibid.
16. Gen. 27.
17. Gen. 6.
18. Matt. 28:1–4, 11–15 NLT.
19. Jer. 31:3.
20. Deut. 33:27.
21. Exod. 34:14.
22. Deut. 4:24.
23. Henri Nouwen, "Running from What We Desire," *Partnership*, July-August 1986, 34–35.
24. Anna Mulrine, "A Godly Approach to Weight Loss," *U.S. News and World Report*, 5 May 1997, 12.
25. Jer. 29:11.
26. Kosner, "Making the Best of Change," 68.
27. Lam. 3:22–24.

Chapter 5: *A Step into Sorrow*

1. 1 Sam. 8:7–8.

Notes

2. 1 Sam. 8:19.
3. Coralee Levine-Shneidman, quoted in Alice Kosner, "Making the Best of Change," *Cosmopolitan,* February 1992, 68.
4. David Hazard, *Early Will I Seek You* (Minneapolis: Bethany House, 1991), 119.
5. Ps. 13:1–2.
6. Job 42:7.
7. Don Allender, "The Hidden Hope in Lament," *Mars Hill Review,* spring 1994, 26.
8. Judy Stewart, "Lament—The Cry to Worship," *Biblical Theology II Tutorial,* 1995, 2.
9. Ibid., 4.
10. Kosner, "Making the Best of Change," *Cosmopolitan,* February 1992, 68.
11. Eugene Peterson, *Living the Message* (San Francisco: HarperSanFrancisco, 1996), 225.
12. Isa. 43:2.
13. James 4:8–10.
14. Arthur Bennett, ed., *The Valley of Vision* (Carlisle, Penn.: Banner of Truth Trust, 1975), 91.
15. Zech. 12:10; 13:1–2.
16. Eccles. 3:1, 4.
17. Isa. 61:2.
18. Jer. 31:13.

Chapter 6: *Finding Peace in the Process*

1. John 16:33.
2. John 16:33 TM.
3. Paul Geisert and Lynda Futrell, "Free Will: A Human, Fuzzy, Chaotic Process," *The Humanist,* May-June 1996, 27.
4. Ibid.
5. "Maintaining Chaos in the Face of Order," *Science News* 147 (24 June 1995), 394.
6. Rom. 8:28 NASB.
7. Matt. 10:29–31.
8. Lev. 24:12; Matt. 26:39; Mark 14:36.
9. Gen. 2:9.
10. Henri Nouwen, *Here and Now: Living in the Spirit* (New York: Crossroads, 1994), 81–82.

Chapter 7: *Learning to Let Go*

1. Carol Kuykendall, *Learning to Let Go* (Wheaton: Tyndale, 1991), 25.
2. Ibid.
3. Laurie Drake, "Conquering Chaos," *Elle* magazine, August 1996, 174–75.

Notes

4. John Briggs and F. David Peat, *Turbulent Mirror: An Illustrated Guide to Chaos Theory and the Science of Wholeness* (New York: Harper and Row, 1989), 22.
5. Ibid., 15.
6. Ibid., 31.
7. Ibid., 178.
8. Ibid.
9. Ibid.
10. Col. 1:15–17, emphasis added.
11. Briggs and Peat, *Turbulent Mirror*, 178.
12. Deborah Shelton, "The Power to Change," *Essence*, January 1996, 80.
13. Ibid.
14. Ibid.
15. Susan L. Taylor, "The Flow of Life," *Essence*, June 1994, 59.
16. Kuykendall, *Learning to Let Go*, 84.

Chapter 8: *Integrating Daily Chaos into the Fabric of Life*

1. William L. Ditto, "Maintaining Chaos in the Face of Order," *Science News* 147 (24 June 1995), 394.
2. I. Peterson, "Disorder to Nudge Order out of Chaos," *Science News* 148 (9 December 1995), 389.
3. Robert E. Cooley, "Signposts at the Dothan Dig," *Christianity Today*, 11 February 1991, 13.
4. Matt. 6:34.
5. Paul Geisert and Lynda Futrell, "Free Will: A Human, Fuzzy, Chaotic Process," *The Humanist*, May-June 1996, 28.
6. Leonard Foley, O.F.M., "Living in Harmony with God's Will," *Care Notes* (Abbey Press, 1990), 5.
7. Ibid., 6.
8. John Briggs and F. David Peat, *Turbulent Mirror: An Illustrated Guide to Chaos Theory and the Science of Wholeness* (New York: Harper and Row, 1989), 147.
9. Ibid., 144.
10. Lam. 3:23.
11. Isa. 43:18–19.

Chapter 9: *Integrating Traumatic Chaos into the Fabric of Life*

1. John 17:4.
2. 2 Cor. 6:4–10 TM.
3. J. Huggins, *A Wolf Story* (Eugene, Oreg.: Harvest House, 1993), 75.
4. Dr. John Trent, "Charting Where You've Been and Where You're Going," *Focus on the Family*, September 1994, 5.
5. Acts 9.
6. Trent, "Charting Where You've Been and Where You're Going," 5.

Notes

7. Henri Nouwen, *Here and Now: Living in the Spirit* (New York: Crossroads, 1994), 43.
8. 2 Peter 1:3–4.
9. 2 Sam. 7:18–19, 22.
10. Isa. 40:11.
11. Isa. 50:4–7.
12. Ruth Myers, *Thirty-One Days of Praise* (Sisters, Oreg.: Multnomah Books, Questar Publishers, 1994), 6.

Chapter 10: *Integrating Chaos through Change Management in the Workplace*

1. Sharon Johnson, "Executive Stress," *U.S. Air* magazine, January 1997, 18.
2. Ibid.
3. John Briggs and F. David Peat, *Turbulent Mirror: An Illustrated Guide to Chaos Theory and the Science of Wholeness* (New York: Harper and Row, 1989), 178.
4. Kim McManus, "Leadership in a Restorative Age," *Nation's Cities Weekly*, 3 April 1995, 8.
5. Ibid.
6. Joseph M. Arceri, "Surviving Change: Playing Organizational Baseball," Praxis Consulting Group, 2.
7. Dr. Adele Scheele, "Coping with Ageism," *Working Woman*, February 1994, 44.
8. Ibid., 2.
9. Johnson, "Executive Stress," 18.
10. Gabriele Lusser Rico, *Writing the Natural Way* (Los Angeles: Tarcher Inc., 1983), 29.
11. Briggs and Peat, *Turbulent Mirror*, 178.
12. Ibid.
13. Arceri, "Surviving Change," 2.
14. Johnson, "Executive Stress," 18.

Chapter 11: *Finding Rest in the Midst of Chaos*

1. Gen. 2:2–3.
2. Heb. 4:9–11.
3. John 17:13.
4. Joe Stowell, *Shepherding the Church into the Twenty-First Century*.
5. John 11.
6. Deut. 33:12.

BOOKS BY LINDA:

Investing Your Life in Things That Matter–Revised,
(WinePress Publishers, 2006)
Resource Guide for Women's Ministry–Revised,
(Broadman & Holman, 2005)
Called to Influence,
(John Maxwell's Injoy, Inc., 2004)
Prayers Jesus Prayed Study Guide,
(Servant Publications, 2002)
Dancing in the Storm: Hope in the Midst of Chaos,
(Revel/Baker Book House, 1999)
Investing Your Life in Things That Matter,
(Broadman & Holman, 1997)
The Strength of a Woman,
(Broadman & Holman, 1996)
The Bible Answers Questions Children Ask,
(Broadman Press, 1992)
Resource Guide for Women's Ministries,
(Broadman Press, 1990)
Women in the Word Bible Study Series:
(Baker Book House, 1995-1998)
    Seeing Jesus: Study of the Letters of Peter & John
    Equipped for Life: Study of Ephesians, Philippians & Colossians
    Saying Yes to God: Study of Esther
    Walking With Jesus: Study of Luke
    Receiving Righteousness in Christ: Study of Romans
    Feeling the Holy Spirit's Power: Study of Acts

CONTRIBUTOR AND TOPICAL NOTE AUTHOR BY LINDA:

NKJV Woman's Study Bible-Book of Romans,
(Thomas Nelson Publishers, 1995)

BOOKS EDITED BY LINDA:

Bringing in the Kingdom: Matthew, Joanne Ellison,
    edited by Linda McGinn Waterman, (self-published, 2015)
Camp Heritage: A Grandparent's Legacy, Pat Vanderhorst,
    edited by Linda McGinn Waterman (Xulon Publishers, 2010)

Linda McGinn Waterman challenges readers, listeners, and audiences with her biblical perspective and rich variety of experiences. Engaging, entertaining, and insightful, as a popular motivational speaker, Linda is described as "contagiously enthusiastic," and has been providing national seminars and conference programs for more than two decades.

As an award-winning author, Linda is Founder and Executive Director of Refreshed Women (www.refreshedwomen.com), a community of women seeking to "passionately pursue purpose" by using their God-given gifts, skills and abilities. Her desire is to help women discover and apply strategies for navigating the turbulent waters of change to realize their full potential and to tell their stories. The hope is that as a result they discover fun, fellowship, and true fulfillment in every season of life. Among her many accomplishments, in 1995 Linda was awarded the National Religious Broadcaster's Genesis Award for the radio program KeyPoints, which she designed and produced.

Linda's greatest joy is being wife to Reen, mother to Ruthie, John and Cera, mother-in-love to Amy and GrandMom to John, Jr., Caroline, and Wyatt on lovely Kent Island (on the Eastern Shore of Maryland) where the Chesapeake Bay glistens while sailboats drift and glide in the breeze.

Refreshed Women is expanding nationally and looking for women who would like to partner with Refreshed Women to begin a chapter in their area. For more information about ways to be actively involved, contact Linda at:
Email: refreshedwomen@gmail.com
Website: www.refreshedwomen.com
Facebook: Linda McGinn Waterman or Refreshed Women
Twitter: @LindaMWaterman
Google+: Linda Waterman

If you would like Linda to speak at your next conference or women's retreat, please check with Linda for her availability!

Made in the USA
Columbia, SC
27 January 2024

31000986R00114